POSITIVE TEACHIN
SECONDARY S

D0298915

C

Dr Kevin Wheldall is Director of the Centre for Child Study at the University of Birmingham where Dr Frank Merrett is Honorary Research Fellow. They are the authors of *Positive Teaching: the behavioural approach* (1984), the BATPACK (1985) and BATSAC (1988) training packages and numerous research articles.

Effective Classroom Behaviour
Management

POSITIVE TEACHING
IN THE
SECONDARY SCHOOL

KEVIN WHELDALL
and
FRANK MERRETT

with Stephen Houghton

P·C·P
Paul Chapman
Publishing Ltd

First published 1989
Paul Chapman Publishing Ltd
144 Liverpool Road
London
N1 1LA

British Library Cataloguing in Publication Data

Wheldall, Kevin 1949–
   Effective classroom behaviour management: positive
   teaching in the secondary school
   1. England. Secondary schools. Disruptive students.
   Teaching
   I. Title   II. Merrett, Frank   III. Houghton, Stephen
   373.11'02

   ISBN 1-85396-075-6

Printed and bound in Great Britain by
Athenaeum Press Ltd, Newcastle upon Tyne

E F 9 8 7

CONTENTS

Preface

Managing troublesome behaviour in the classroom is a problem faced by all secondary school teachers at some time in their careers. The problem of disruptive behaviour in schools generally, prompted the recent Enquiry into Discipline in Schools chaired by Lord Elton, which was initiated by the Secretary of State for Education in 1988 and to which we gave evidence as expert witnesses. In a sense, this book is a response to the recently published Elton Report, at least in the context of classroom behaviour problems. The Elton Report refers to our research and recommends our package for training teachers in the skills of classroom behaviour management. We believe that problems of disruptive behaviour and indiscipline can be resolved, or at least reduced, by teachers learning to be both more sensitive and more positive in their interactions with young people in secondary schools.

For over ten years we have been researching and disseminating what we refer to as Positive Teaching. This has included an extensive programme of research studies in secondary schools, some of which has involved our former doctoral student, Stephen Houghton, who has helped in the preparation of sections of this book. We have examined the types of classroom behaviour secondary teachers find particularly troublesome and have observed how they commonly react to such behaviour. We have asked schools about their reward and sanction systems and have asked pupils for their views on effective rewards and punishments. Most importantly, we have carried out experiments in secondary schools to determine effective procedures for establishing good, positive classroom behaviour management.

Our programmes of research have greatly influenced our teaching. In order to provide effective training in Positive Teaching, we developed in-service training packages for teachers based on these findings. In 1985 we published our *Behavioural Approach to Teaching Package (BATPACK)* for training primary teachers in classroom behaviour management. This was enthusiastically received. By releasing our package for wider use by other trained tutors we were able to satisfy the needs of more teachers. In response to demand from those working in the secondary sector, we subsequently developed and published a secondary version, *The Behavioural Approach to Teaching Secondary Aged Children (BATSAC) Package*, in 1988.

In this book, we aim to provide an overview of our research and methods for those who have not been on one of our BATSAC courses and a useful summary for those who have. We should emphasise, however, that reading a book about Positive Teaching is no substitute for learning how to go about it. We learn new skills by practising them not by reading about them. The final chapter of this book contains a description of the BATSAC training package, on which this book is based, and we would encourage readers to attend a BATSAC course in order to improve their skills in classroom behaviour management. By using Positive Teaching methods, secondary school teachers can build less stressful and more effective teaching and learning environments. It is really quite straightforward, but for pupil behaviour to change, teachers must first change their own behaviour. This is the hard part but it can be done, as we show in this book.

We would like to thank our students for their enthusiastic support for Positive Teaching over the years. Many of the studies we report were carried out by students working under our supervision. These students have included both mature, experienced teachers on in-service courses and younger, post-graduates on pre-service courses. We would also like to thank the following teachers for their helpful comments on draft chapters of this book: Mary Higgins, Diane Hoban, Paddy Spurgeon, Christopher Spurgeon and Jane Yeomans. We reserve to ourselves all responsibility for any blemishes or omissions that remain. Our final word of thanks is due to John Shearwood for his most valuable help in producing the final manuscript for printing.

Kevin Wheldall and Frank Merrett, Summer, 1989

Chapter One
IDENTIFYING TROUBLESOME CLASSROOM BEHAVIOUR

Reports from the popular newspapers, television and radio might well lead the person in the street to suppose that the behaviours which trouble secondary teachers most in school are those associated with insubordination, opposition and abuse and that many are of a violent nature. The impression we get is that if you are not mugged on your way into school you almost certainly will be on the way out!

For example, the National Association of Schoolmasters/Union of Women Teachers recently sent a questionnaire to all of its 100,000 plus members. The Union's subsequent report, *Pupil Violence and Serious Disorder in Schools* published in 1986, highlights phrases such as "Physical violence: teachers at risk" and "Off duty but not out of danger". It includes accounts by teachers, such as the following, which remind one of tales by Gerard Hoffnung, being veritable catalogues of harassment over a period of some years.

> During the last 14 years I have been assaulted seven times, once with a knife, once with a stiletto, once with an air rifle (when I was shot in the chest), once when a pupil fed gas into my classroom when I was teaching, twice when pupils have attempted to attack me with their fists and once when an ex-pupil tried twice to run me over with a car.

> In the past seven years I have been butted, punched, spat at, and had a javelin thrown at me with such force that whilst it missed me, it penetrated a door. My home and my car have been threatened, as has my wife.

These cases are so extreme that we might be forgiven for smiling at them, perhaps especially at the ordering of priorities in the last line of the second account. These are very rare cases which, thankfully, very few of us will have encountered. There is no doubt, however, that some teachers are subjected to a great deal of stress. Over recent years, teaching has undoubtedly become a more difficult business, requiring greater skill. Nevertheless, it has to be pointed out that the NAS/UWT survey was based on a questionnaire return of only 4,000 (i.e. less than 5% of members). As the union admits, this "may possibly have produced an unrepresentative sample". The small percentage of teachers who replied are likely to have been a self-selected sample of those few who have experienced violence of some sort.

We should also recognise that troublesome behaviour in young people is not a new phenomenon. Take the following two examples.

> Children now love luxury. They have bad manners and contempt for authority. They show disrespect for their elders and love chatter in place of exercise; children are now tyrants, not the servants of their households.

> The world is passing through troubled times. The young people of today think of nothing but themselves. They have no reverence for their parents or for old age. They talk as if they alone know everything and what passes for wisdom with us is foolishness with them. As for the girls, they are foolish and immodest in speech, behaviour and dress.

In reading these words we could easily be listening to the views of some parents and teachers today or perhaps reading a *Daily Telegraph* editorial. But the first statement is attributed to Socrates and the second to Peter the Simple (1274). Clearly, it is important to keep a sense of proportion and to resist the flight into hysteria encouraged by the media.

In society at large a more liberal and generally less authoritarian attitude prevails today than even 20 or 30 years ago. This is reflected, if not actively welcomed, in many schools and many teachers are appreciative of the changed nature of the relationships they now enjoy with pupils. Some teachers are making more of an effort to relate to their pupils in a less authoritarian way and to treat the older ones as young adults. But this has also led to serious challenges to authority for some teachers, perhaps especially those who have been less quick to adapt to the present, more relaxed, climate. Secondary pupils today are less likely to live in fear of their teachers and will be more likely to react if treated harshly or unfairly. These are important considerations for any approach to dealing with disruptive behaviour but before we can go much further we need to consider more carefully the nature of troublesome behaviour. Is the problem of schools really the high incidence of abusive and violent acts or is teacher stress caused by other forms of pupil behaviour? This was one of the questions addressed by the Elton Report (1989), *Discipline in Schools.*

Which classroom behaviours do secondary teachers say they find most troublesome?

Children with behaviour problems are a common type of referral to educational psychologists, and teachers frequently cite classroom behaviour problems as one of their major difficulties. However, there has been surprisingly little research concerned to identify the behaviours which classroom teachers find most troublesome. Various studies have attempted to determine prevalence rates of troublesome behaviour in children but the variation in reported incidence is considerable, varying from about 5% to over 25%. It is clear either that behaviour problems fluctuate unpredictably in incidence or, more likely, the definition of behaviour problems varies considerably across studies. Our own concern has been with identifying what teachers regard as troublesome behaviour in the classroom. We were interested to know not only what proportion of secondary aged children are behaviourally troublesome to teachers but also just what these troublesome behaviours are.

Before describing our research there are several important aspects of the problem of classroom behaviour that we need to consider. First, there is the question of emphasis. Previous research has tended to be concerned almost exclusively with identifying the incidence of children with behaviour problems. Consequently, the children have been the focus, rather than the behaviour. Our emphasis is upon the behaviour itself. Second, there is the need to define and describe the relevant behaviours which make up the rag-bag category of troublesome behaviour. If we use vague, catch-all phrases we must not be surprised if we find variations in incidence. Moreover, what is disturbing to one teacher may be quite acceptable to another, which emphasises the importance of objective definition of an array of specific behaviours which teachers may find troublesome. Third, there is the question of the severity of the problem behaviour as against the rate at which it occurs. There is no doubt that an incident of stabbing in the classroom is to be regarded as extremely severe but, thankfully, such events are rare. On the other hand, a relatively trivial offence such as calling out may occur so frequently that the lesson dissolves into total chaos. So it is necessary to consider both the degree of troublesomeness and the frequency of problem behaviours.

We attempted to determine what teachers themselves believed to be the most frequent and the most troublesome disruptive behaviours occurring in secondary school classrooms. Teachers completed (anonymously) a questionnaire which sought information on their age, sex, subject specialism and length of teaching experience. We then asked them to focus on the class they taught most frequently and to indicate the age level and size of that class. The questionnaire then posed a series of questions related to classroom behaviour problems. The first asked, "Do you feel that you spend more time dealing with problems of order and control than you ought?" The next three questions were concerned with identifying which of the ten categories of disruptive behaviour listed in the table below were a) most frequent and b) most troublesome. This was first asked in general terms and then with reference to individual children selected by each teacher as being particularly troublesome.

The questionnaire was distributed to six secondary schools from one West Midlands Local Education Authority on a 30% stratified random sample basis. Sufficient survey forms were sent to every school in the sample so that each full-time class teacher could complete the questionnaire. Replies were received from all six schools involved, resulting in a 62% return rate of questionnaires. Of the 251 teachers replying 45% were women and all age ranges were represented. The sample was distributed fairly evenly over the range of ages taught and included all subject specialisms.

Over half of our sample (55%) responded affirmatively to the question "Do you think that you spend more time on problems of order and control than you ought?" A higher percentage (61%) of women than men (50%) responded in this way. Higher percentages (72%) of teachers of modern languages and science responded affirmatively, compared with teachers of craft design technology (43%) and physical education (44%).

The categories of misbehaviour employed in the secondary survey

A	Verbal abuse	Making offensive or insulting remarks to staff or other pupils likely to lead to confrontation (as distinct from D below).
B	Making unnecessary noise (non-verbal)	Banging objects/doors, scraping chairs, moving clumsily.
C	Disobedience	Refusing/failing to carry out instructions or to keep class or school rules.
D	Talking out of turn	Calling out, making remarks, interrupting and distracting others by talking or chattering.
E	Idleness/slowness	Slow to begin or finish work, small amount of work completed.
F	Unpunctuality	Late to school/lessons, late in from playtime/break.
G	Hindering other children	Distracting others from their work, interfering with their equipment or materials.
H	Physical aggression	Poking, pushing, striking others, throwing things.
I	Untidiness	In appearance, in written work, in classroom, in desks.
J	Out of seat	Getting out of seat without permission, wandering around.

The average class size taught was 21. On average 4.1 pupils were regarded as troublesome by their class teachers and of these 2.7 were boys. Again, modern language teachers reported a higher than average number of troublesome pupils per class (6.3) whereas remedial and craft design technology teachers reported lower than average rates (3.1). The mean number of pupils per class regarded as troublesome also varied according to pupil age. As the age of the class reported on increased the mean number of girls found to be troublesome declined. Generally, this was also true for boys, except for the fifth year, where an increase was evident.

Asked to pick out the two most troublesome, individual children in the classes, boys were identified as the most troublesome by 76% and as the next most troublesome by 77%. Teachers in all academic faculties selected a higher percentage of boys than girls as being the most troublesome but there was considerable variability. For example, 93% of modern languages teachers selected boys as being the most troublesome compared with only 55% of mathematics teachers. Boys were clearly more troublesome than girls in the first two years of secondary education and by year five some 86% of teachers regarded boys as the most troublesome individuals. This supports the anecdotal view that boys, generally, tend to be more troublesome than girls.

What was it that these pupils did that was troublesome? As we said earlier, it was the type and frequency of troublesome behaviours in which we were particularly interested. When asked to pick out the most *troublesome* behaviour 50% of secondary teachers cited talking out of turn (TOOT) and 17% cited hindering other children (HOC). (A further 13% cited idleness/slowness.) None of the other categories reached over 10%, as the bar graph on page 7 shows. Generally, the findings were similar across academic faculties and according to the age of children taught, with minor variations. It is interesting to note, however, that idleness/slowness was apparently not a problem behaviour with first year pupils but increased in severity with the older age groups. In fact, 26% of teachers cited it as being troublesome by year five.

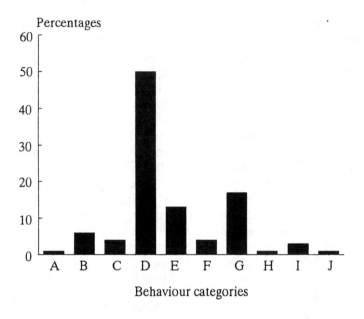

Percentages

Behaviour categories

Most troublesome behaviours

The findings for the most *frequent* troublesome behaviours gave a broadly similar picture and when we went on to ask about the troublesome behaviours of individual children, again we got the same response, TOOT followed by HOC. These two categories are not particularly serious misbehaviours. The category physical aggression was cited by only two teachers (less than 1%) as being the most troublesome behaviour and came tenth (last) in rank order. Similarly, only three teachers cited verbal abuse as the most troublesome behaviour. Physical violence and verbal abuse appear to be problems encountered by relatively few teachers but many, if not most, have their job made more stressful by the petty misbehaviours which we have identified. Even for the most troublesome children the key behaviours identified were not particularly serious or problematic.

In passing we should note that a parallel survey we conducted with primary school teachers reached very similar conclusions, TOOT and HOC again being selected as the most troublesome behaviours. Contrary to popular belief, secondary school pupils are not necessarily more badly behaved but, in fact, continue to display many of the same troublesome behaviours as at primary school.

What may we conclude from these results? We would appear to be safe in assuming that the classroom behaviour problems experienced by most secondary school teachers are not of a serious nature. TOOT and HOC appear to be the two misbehaviours which teachers generally identify as causing them the most trouble and as occurring most often. These findings are broadly confirmed by the larger scale replication study commissioned for the Elton Report which was inspired by our research. This is not to say that serious incidents do not occur occasionally in some schools but they are certainly not as frequent as the media would have us believe. Physical violence appears to be a problem encountered (thankfully) by relatively few teachers but many, if not most, teachers have their job made more stressful by the petty misbehaviours we have identified.

Regarding the prevalence of children identified as troublesome, we may relate the figures from our survey to the prevalence rates referred to earlier. On average, 4.1 children per class (of average class size 21) were said by their teachers to be troublesome. This yields a prevalence rate of nearly 20% which falls within the estimates we cited previously. This figure should be appreciated in the context of the behaviour categories which teachers selected. Even for the most troublesome children the key behaviours identified were not particularly serious or problematic.

To sum up, the behaviour problems that secondary teachers encounter may vary to some degree from district to district, school to school and from individual to individual but the results from our survey suggest that there is a consensus of opinion among teachers. The majority are bothered by the behaviour of some of their pupils but the most common and troublesome behaviours are relatively trivial. None of the key troublesome behaviours are serious crimes but they are time-wasting, irritating, stressful and, ultimately, exhausting for teachers. They are the kinds of behaviours which elicit the litany of reprimands and desist commands heard so frequently in classrooms. The good news is that these are the very behaviours which respond well to simple, positive methods of classroom behaviour management as we will show in this book.

Causes of troublesome behaviour

In our view there has been an excessive pre-occupation with the so-called causes of misbehaviour. Teachers and parents are often very quick to give reasons why they think young people misbehave in class even if, as is usually the case, they are only guessing. The reasons teachers commonly give for difficult behaviour can be thought of in a number of ways depending on whether they see the reason as being somehow within the pupils themselves, stemming from their home backgrounds or the kind of neighbourhood in which they are living or, perhaps, from their school or classroom situations. In the table below we give examples of the sort of reasons sometimes given for talking out of turn (TOOT) and hindering other children (HOC), according to these categories.

Behaviour problem	Causes within the pupil	Causes within the family or neighbourhood	Causes within the school or class setting
TOOT	extraverted a bit thick neurotic	large family poor diet TV always on	work too easy directions unclear seating
HOC	aggressive brain-damaged insecure	violent father council housing spoilt at home	lack of space poor teaching no clear rules

In our view, many of the causes or reasons given in the first two columns do not bear close scrutiny. To say that Darren interferes with the work of others because he is aggressive does not get us very far. It is a label which merely substitutes different words to describe the behaviour. We call such labels given for troublesome behaviours *explanatory fictions*. Take the following conversation between two teachers, for example,

> "Jenny Stevens has always got a lot to say for herself. Rabbit, rabbit, rabbit - she never stops talking! I wish I knew why."

> "Well, you see, the reason is that Jenny is a classic extravert, that's why."

> "How do you know that?"

> "It's obvious. Extraverts are very sociable types who like to talk a lot."

This is just a circular argument and gets nowhere. Giving a fancy label to a misbehaviour does not help us to solve the problem. Some educational psychologists have been irritating teachers by doing this sort of thing for years!

Some reasons given may be all too real but there is little that we as teachers can do about such causes. Jenny may watch too many video nasties, eat too much junk food, come from a family of seven, have an unresolved Electra complex and/or be suffering from minimal brain damage but there is little that we can do directly to resolve any of these difficulties even if they are influencing her classroom behaviour. We cannot ask Jenny to hop on the couch and tell us about her dreams nor would advice to her parents on birth control or healthy eating be very effective. We are teachers not social workers or psychiatrists. We do best to concentrate on reasons where we have very much more positive control.

To take this position is not to deny the importance of, nor to deny the interest of the teacher in, the home or in co-operation with parents but we must accept our limitations. Similarly, we accept that pupils' personal problems will sometimes affect their behaviour in school. We, as teachers, know from personal experience how our day's work in schools can be affected by, say, an argument at breakfast time. Clearly, sympathy for and an understanding of the personal and social difficulties of pupils are essential characteristics of caring, positive teachers but these may not be enough. Whilst we cannot necessarily do much to alleviate personal problems or counter the effects of poor social conditions, we can strive to create positive, responsive environments for pupils in our classrooms where we have more control over many of the elements. Such environments would provide warmth and acceptance within a climate of clear rules and expectations and opportunities for engaging in activities which provide positive feedback.

If we look back at the third column in our table we can see that many of these possible causes of misbehaviour are amenable to resolution by action on the part of the teachers. We can make sure that the work we set is at an appropriate level. We can negotiate with our pupils some effective, positive rules for appropriate conduct in the classroom. We can ensure that the seating arrangements are suitable for the work we have set and that we use the space available to the best advantage. We can learn to be more observant of pupil behaviour, both good and bad, and to respond to it appropriately. Positive teachers realise that they have a great deal of control over key factors in the classroom. This is not always used as effectively as it might be by many teachers and in this book we will discuss how Positive Teaching methods may be employed to resolve classroom behaviour difficulties.

The five principles of Positive Teaching

Positive Teaching is based on five basic principles. The aim is to promote good classroom practice by, almost exclusively, positive methods. Our concern in this book is with effective classroom behaviour management but this is not meant to imply that Positive Teaching does not have an equally important role to play in teaching academic skills such as reading and writing. We will be concerned here, however, exclusively with the use of Positive Teaching methods to manage pupils' social behaviour. We should note, however, that it is generally accepted that appropriate behaviour in the classroom is necessary for academic learning to take place. Secondary pupils will have little opportunity to learn if they are continually being disrupted or if they themselves are continually disrupting the teacher or other pupils.

1. Teaching is concerned with the observable.

Positive teachers concern themselves with what pupils actually do rather than speculating about unconscious motives or processes which may be thought to underlie their pupils' behaviour. The only evidence we have about what people can do or will do and about what they believe comes to us by observing their behaviour. Consequently, careful definition and observation of behaviour are central to the behavioural approach. As we have already noted, teachers frequently propose explanations for behaviour which are not reasons at all but merely labels or explanatory fictions. To say that Barry or Imran is often out of his seat because he is hyperactive is, quite simply, circular and gets us nowhere; the expression hyperactive is just another word to describe the same behaviour. It does nothing to explain it and provides no help in solving the problem. Indeed, such labels are often used as an excuse for doing nothing.

2. Almost all classroom behaviour is learned.

Positive teachers do not deny genetic inheritance nor do they assume that anybody can be taught to do anything given time. Genetic inheritance may set the limits for what an individual can learn, but behaviour is still the result of learning. Certainly this applies to the sort of behaviour that teachers are chiefly concerned with, such as knowing how to respond politely to others or being able to read. Of course, pupils learn bad behaviour as well as good behaviour. The good news is that bad behaviour can be unlearned and new, more appropriate behaviour learned in its place.

3. Learning involves change in behaviour.

The only way that we know (that we can know) that learning has taken place is by observing change in a pupil's behaviour. Positive teachers will not be satisfied with vague statements such as, "Gemma has a better attitude towards school now". Evidence is needed that she now attends on time, answers more questions, completes her homework or whatever. These are all clear examples of behaviours which can, if necessary, be counted and compared.

4. Behaviour changes as a result of its consequences.

This means that we all (pupils and teachers) learn on the basis of tending to repeat behaviours which are followed by consequences we find desirable or rewarding. We tend not to repeat behaviours, the consequences of which we find aversive or punishing. If we wish to change the behaviour of our pupils we should concentrate upon arranging for desirable consequences to follow appropriate behaviour. It has been shown repeatedly that rewarding appropriate behaviour is more effective than punishing undesirable behaviour.

5. Behaviours are also influenced by classroom contexts.

In any situation some behaviours are more appropriate than others. If a pupil's behaviour is appropriate for a particular circumstance then it is likely to be rewarded by the people (adults or peers) who are around. If it is inappropriate to the situation it is less likely to be rewarded and may even be punished. As a result pupils rapidly learn not only how to behave in certain ways but also when and where such behaviours are appropriate. Certain behaviours are more likely in some situations rather than others simply because there is more opportunity to engage in them. For example, there is far more chance to chatter and to interfere with others when seated in classroom table groups than when in rows. It is necessary to consider classroom antecedents for behaviour as well as consequences. We will consider these aspects in more detail later.

These five principles sum up what we mean by Positive Teaching. The main assumption is that pupils' behaviour is primarily learned and maintained as a result of their interactions with their environment, which includes other pupils and teachers. Consequently, behaviour can be changed by altering certain features of that environment. As we have said, the key environmental features are events which immediately precede or follow behaviour. This means that classroom behaviours followed by consequences which the pupils find rewarding will tend to increase in frequency. Similarly, certain changes in behaviour may be brought about merely by changing the classroom setting.

If we believe that teaching is concerned with helping pupils to learn new skills and gain new information, and if we believe also that learning implies a change or changes in behaviour, then it follows logically that teaching is about changing behaviour. If teaching is about changing behaviour then the role of the teacher is, quite simply, to bring about changes in the behaviour of the pupils in his or her class.

Justifying our actions

But what right have we to play God? How can we justify our actions when seeking to change pupils' behaviour? Questions such as these cannot be shirked; if we do not ask them of ourselves, then sooner or later someone else will.

The first point we can make is that Positive Teaching is honest and straightforward in so far as it encourages teachers to examine a troublesome problem, to define it clearly, to state their aims and the means by which they are attempting to bring about change. Before teachers can decide whether they need to take action over a certain behaviour they must decide upon the appropriateness of it in the classroom context. Teachers must be able to justify their actions in terms of the long-term benefits for their pupils. Some pupil behaviour may be annoying to the teacher but not, in itself, harmful. For example, chewing in class, though it may be judged to be disrespectful by some teachers, could not be said to be wrong, unless dietary or other considerations are taken into account. If we can agree that the teacher's main task is to arrange for learning to take place, then within the context of the classroom any behaviour can be judged inappropriate if it:

1. interferes with the child's own learning,

2. interferes with the learning of other members of the class or,

3. prevents the teacher from getting on with his or her job of instructing, explaining, reading, organising, coaching and so on.

Thus day-dreaming, playing with materials or apparatus or wandering around the room would certainly interfere with the pupil's own learning. Talking to others in the group or attacking them or their property would clearly interfere with the learning of others, whilst persistent conduct of this nature would probably demand a great deal of the teacher's time and attention, preventing much effective teaching from going on. Much of the teacher's concern is to see that the children concentrate or get on with the job in hand; what is known as *on-task* behaviour. If the pupils are not on-task then the likelihood is that not much learning is going on. In fact, recent research has shown a clear relationship between on-task behaviour and the amount of classwork completed. If we can increase on-task behaviour then at least learning is possible, providing always that the material is appropriate to the pupil's current skill level. The main aim of this book is with the management of children's classroom behaviour, which inevitably yields improved academic behaviour.

Some critics might argue that Positive Teaching merely attempts to treat the symptoms (the behaviour) rather than the underlying problem itself. Such approaches, they claim, are akin to prescribing aspirin for toothache, which alleviates the symptoms (pain) but leaves the real cause (a rotten tooth) untreated. As a result of this, they would argue, other symptoms (problems) will inevitably surface sooner or later. In classroom terms this would be illustrated by a child who, when taught to remain seated instead of wandering about the classroom, will now begin calling out to the teacher or displaying other unwanted behaviours, since the cause is left untreated. This is sometimes referred to as symptom substitution. In response to this, we would argue that:

1. the behaviour is the problem

2. supposedly deeper causes are frequently difficult to identify and often take the form of explanatory fictions, and

3. there is no experimental evidence to suggest that if we remove one problem another one will appear to replace it.

In sum Positive Teaching concerns itself with the observable. There are no inner mysteries, the approach is direct and the outcomes clear. In the final analysis we point to our success rate in achieving enduring changes in behaviour without any evidence for symptom substitution or any other side-effects.

Finally, there is the issue of so-called bribery. Because rewards and praise are important parts of the Positive Teaching repertoire, the charge of bribery is sometimes levelled at our approach. This glib charge is easily challenged since bribery usually means to give someone an inducement in advance to do something immoral or illegal! In Positive Teaching praise and rewards are, essentially, given following appropriate behaviour which the teacher has determined is in the pupil's long-term interests. To call such behaviour bribery makes as much sense as saying that teachers have to be bribed for working with a monthly pay cheque!

Further reading

Our survey of troublesome classroom behaviour in secondary schools is reported fully in:

Houghton, S., Wheldall, K. and Merrett, F. (1988). Classroom behaviour problems which secondary teachers say they find most troublesome. *British Educational Research Journal, 14,* 295-310.

For a broad perspective on the question of disruptive behaviour in schools teachers should consult the Elton Report:

Department of Education and Science (1989). *Discipline in Schools.* London: H.M.S.O.

Chapter Two
FOCUSING ON APPROPRIATE
CLASSROOM BEHAVIOUR

Problems of classroom behaviour and poor motivation are endemic in education. Teachers consistently cite difficulties in these two areas as their main classroom concerns and traditionally they have been dealt with in the same way, that is, by punitive methods. Both unacceptable or troublesome behaviour and idleness or lack of interest represent threats to the teacher's role which he or she commonly seeks to prevent by aversive means. One consequence of this may be the daily repetition of desist commands heard in many classrooms: "Sit down, Nadia. Talking again, Narinder. Leave Brendon alone, Nigel - get on with your own work. Something of interest outside, Mary? Eyes on your work please," and so on, endlessly. Teachers become very good at noticing and commenting on the disruptive behaviour of their pupils (in a sense they feel forced to do so) and for a number of reasons they feel that they have to respond.

Teachers the world over spend a considerable proportion of their teaching time reprimanding pupils for troublesome and/or non work-related behaviours as we shall see. They hardly ever comment approvingly on appropriate behaviour. As we have already shown, teachers are mostly concerned with high frequency but relatively trivial troublesome behaviours such as talking out of turn and hindering other pupils . These are the behaviours which help to cause teacher stress as they occur with monotonous regularity and result in immediate reaction which usually takes the form of reprimands and sanctions. We believe that teachers should *act* rather than *react* in the classroom. To react on the spur of the moment may be natural; but is it professional and is it effective? This surely is the difference between a professional and a lay response to the behaviour of a young person.

The phasing out of corporal punishment in our schools has been accompanied by renewed interest in seeking out alternative methods of achieving good classroom discipline. In our research on Positive Teaching we have concentrated on how teachers should behave in classrooms in order to bring about suitable conditions for effective and efficient learning to take place. We have been concerned with problems of troublesome classroom behaviour and with methods of encouraging pupils to behave in ways which will maximise their opportunities for learning appropriate academic skills and knowledge. We have shown teachers how to encourage and increase the kinds of behaviour they want to see their pupils engaged in and which are of educational benefit to them. In order to do this, teachers need to know more about behaviour, its antecedents and its consequences.

The ABC of Positive Teaching

The crucial elements of Positive Teaching are as simple as ABC.

A refers to the antecedent conditions, i.e. the context in which a behaviour occurs or what is happening in that environment prior to a behaviour occurring.

B refers to the behaviour itself, i.e. what a pupil is actually doing in real physical terms (not what you think he or she is doing as a result of inferences from his or her behaviour).

C refers to the consequences of the behaviour, i.e. what happens to the pupil after the behaviour.

Let us look at these three elements again in a little more detail, beginning with behaviour. We will return to the topic of antecedents in Chapter Three.

Behaviour. We have already said that pupils' behaviour refers to what they are actually doing and positive teachers attempt to say what they are doing in as precise a way as possible. If we observe a pupil looking at a book, we would not write down studying since another observer or someone else reading our notes might interpret studying differently. It is too vague and imprecise. We might record that the pupil was looking at the book and turned over five pages in a period of three minutes but to say that this is studying is to interpret. Such interpretation is prone to inaccuracy and vagueness and is unlikely to be useful. Similarly, if a teacher tells us that Jason is always "messing about" in class, we have to ask the teacher to define that behaviour more clearly. What we regard as messing about may not be what the teacher regards as messing about. Moreover, if we use a vague definition there is no guarantee that it is the same sort of behaviour we are categorising in this way two days running. So we would ask the teacher to list any of Jason's behaviours which he or she finds objectionable and then to define them as precisely as possible. This is known as *pin-pointing*.

As we have seen, talking out of turn is frequently found at the top of many teachers' lists of troublesome behaviours. If we define this as "any non work-related talking by pupils when the teacher has requested the class to get on with set work quietly", then we are moving closer towards an objective definition. The more objective our definition, the easier it is for two observers to agree that a certain behaviour has occurred and the easier it is to count instances of such behaviour. Counting instances of behaviour is an extremely important component of Positive Teaching because comparison of such counts allows us to see what is happening when we try to bring about change over a period of time. Precise definition of behaviour also helps us to avoid the danger of over-interpretation and giving explanatory fictions as causes of behaviour. These are generally unhelpful and give a veneer or gloss of scientific explanation.

Consequences. As we said earlier, this refers to the fact that we (and that means all of us, pupils and teachers alike) tend to repeat behaviours which bring us what we want and to refrain from repeating behaviours leading to events which we want to avoid. Almost everyone finds praise and approval rewarding and will tend to behave in a way which is likely to be followed by praise or approval. A major concern within Positive Teaching is with the identification of items and events which pupils find rewarding and to structure the teaching environment so as to make access to these rewards dependent upon behaviour which the teacher wants to encourage in class. This is what we mean by acting rather than reacting.

In simple everyday language consequences may be described as rewarding or punishing. Rewarding consequences, which we call *positive reinforcers*, are events which we seek out or "go for", whilst we try to avoid *punishing* consequences. Neutral consequences are events which affect us neither way. Behaviours followed by positive reinforcers are likely to increase in frequency. Behaviours followed by punishers tend to decrease in frequency whilst neutral consequences have no effect. In Positive Teaching, infrequent but appropriate behaviours (for example, getting on with the set work quietly) are made more frequent by arranging for positive reinforcers, such as teacher attention and approval, to follow their occurrence. In the environment of the classroom the teacher is responsible for providing many of the consequences for the behaviour of pupils. Teachers do this in a number of ways but chiefly by responding to their pupils' behaviour and their work in terms of feedback, through words and actions. This is called social reinforcement.

Undesired behaviours may be decreased in frequency by ensuring that positive reinforcers do not follow their occurrence, i.e. a neutral consequence is arranged. Occasionally it may be necessary to follow undesired behaviours with punishers (for example, a quiet reprimand) in an attempt to reduce the frequency of behaviour rapidly but there are many problems associated with this procedure. Punishment plays only a minor and infrequent role in Positive Teaching not least because sometimes what we believe to be punishing is, in fact, reinforcing to the pupil. Pupils who receive little attention from adults may behave in ways which result in adult disapproval. Such pupils may prefer disapproval to being ignored and will continue to behave like this because adult attention, in itself, whether praise or reprimand, is positively reinforcing. This is what some people call attention-seeking behaviour.

We should note that terminating a punishing consequence is also reinforcing and can be, and often is, used to increase desired behaviours. This is known as *negative reinforcement*. Again this has problems associated with its use since pupils may rapidly learn other, more effective, ways of avoiding the negative consequence than you had in mind. For example, some teachers continually use sarcasm and ridicule with their pupils. They cease only when their pupils behave as they wish. Another way for pupils to avoid this unpleasant consequence, however, other than by doing as the teacher wishes, is to skip that lesson or stay away from school.

Finally, one can punish by removing or terminating positive consequences (for example, by taking away privileges). This is known as *response cost* but again there are similar problems associated with this. Pupils may find alternative ways of avoiding this unpleasant consequence. Lying, cheating and shifting the blame are common strategies employed. These are all behaviours we would wish to discourage but by creating consequences which we believe to be aversive we may be making them more likely to occur.

When we want to teach pupils to do something new, or to encourage them to behave in a certain way more frequently than they normally do, it is important that we ensure that they are positively reinforced every time they behave as we want them to. This normally leads to rapid learning and is known as continuous reinforcement. When they have learned the new behaviour and/or are behaving as we want them to do regularly, then we may maintain this behaviour more economically by reducing the frequency of reinforcement.

Another important reason for wanting to reduce the frequency of reinforcement is that pupils may become less responsive if the positive reinforcer becomes too easily available. Consequently, once pupils are regularly behaving in an appropriate way we can best maintain that behaviour by ensuring that they are now reinforced only intermittently. Intermittent reinforcement can be arranged so that pupils are reinforced every so often (i.e. in terms of time) or, alternatively, after so many occurrences of the behaviour. These different ways of organising the frequency of reinforcement are known as reinforcement schedules and we need to bear these considerations in mind when we are applying the principles of Positive Teaching in the classroom. We shall consider these points again in Chapter Five.

With some pupils the behaviour that concerns us has not yet been learned, so our job is to teach it. With others, the behaviour is learned but does not occur frequently enough. Other pupils frequently behave in inappropriate ways. Positive Teaching is about changing the frequency of behaviour. It can be used to teach new skills or to increase or decrease existing rates of behaviour. It is important to emphasise that Positive Teaching is primarily concerned with increasing the frequency of appropriate behaviour in the classroom rather than with reducing disruptive behaviour *per se*. In a sense, this leads to the same outcome. Since a person can engage in only one sort of activity at a time, if we increase the time spent profitably, we must reduce the opportunities for misbehaviour.

It should also be emphasised that Positive Teaching is not about creating robots who just do as they are told, mindlessly following the teacher's instructions. Rather, Positive Teaching is about helping pupils to become effective independent learners. We certainly do not advocate approaches requiring rigid adherence to curricula based on behavioural objectives, for example, as we have argued elsewhere, in the book, *Effective Classroom Learning*. Positive teachers should, in effect, like all good teachers, have the ultimate aim of making themselves redundant.

How do secondary teachers typically behave in the classroom?

Teachers are in general agreement with the view that, where possible, their interactions with pupils should be positive, involving the use of praise, rather than negative, involving the use of reprimands. This is altogether more agreeable for both teachers and pupils. Nobody thrives in a situation where one party is always chiding the other and where conflict remains barely concealed beneath the surface.

In a recent survey of opinion we carried out among secondary teachers we found that all of them agreed that it is better to be encouraging towards pupils rather than to nag and chide them. Indeed, a common reaction to our suggestion to teachers that they should improve their use of praise and encouragement is, "Ah, but we do that already". Of the teachers in the survey mentioned above, 90% thought that they were more positive than negative in dealing with their pupils. We wanted to know whether this belief was, in fact, true and how far this common attitude was carried through in teachers' behaviour. In other words, do they use more praise than blame?

Consequently, we arranged for a large sample of British secondary school teachers to be observed interacting with their classes in comprehensive schools in the West Midlands. Our trained observers, using specially prepared observation schedules, watched 130 secondary teachers teaching pupils aged 11 to 16. Teachers and their classes were observed at different times during the day and week on at least three separate occasions for half an hour.

Our observation schedule entitled OPTIC (Observing Pupils and Teachers In Classrooms) samples teachers' use of praise and disapproval and the behaviour of their classes. Observers record the number of times teachers give praise or reprimands to pupils and whether these are in response to pupils' academic work or their social behaviour. The schedule also allows an estimate to be made of the amount of time pupils spend behaving appropriately; for example, actually getting on with the work set by the teacher (or time on-task, as we call it).

The good news is that, on average, this sample of secondary pupils spent about 80% of their time on-task and this is in line with the estimates of other observers. (It may be compared with only 70% in a similar sample of primary classes we observed.) Two thirds of the secondary classes spent between 65% and 95% of their time engaged in activities defined as appropriate by their teachers.

Overall, teachers were much more positive than negative in their responses to pupils' academic work (see the table on page 24). On average teachers used three times as much praise as disapproval. When commenting on pupils' classroom behaviour, however, teachers used three times as much disapproval as approval. Approval for social behaviour was very rare; 26 (20%) of the teachers observed gave none at all. Pupils are clearly expected to behave well and are continually reprimanded if they do not. In our view, much of this negative responding to classroom behaviour by teachers is ineffective and may, in fact, be counter-productive.

Approval to and disapproval of academic work and classroom behaviour expressed as percentages of all teacher responses

	Approval to	Disapproval of	Totals
Academic work	45	15	60
Classroom behaviour	10	30	40
Totals	55	45	100

First year classes received most approval but this declined steadily with increased pupil age. The highest levels of on-task behaviour (around 88%) were also recorded in first year classes.

The only major difference we found between the behaviour of male and female teachers was in their use of disapproval for classroom behaviour. Women teachers clearly disapproved of their pupils' behaviour more often than their male colleagues. In our sample, maths teachers were found to be the most positive and teachers of modern languages the most negative. Interestingly enough, as a broad generalisation, the lowest average levels of on-task behaviour were found in modern language classes and the highest in maths classes. We should also recall that this ties in with our earlier evidence that a high proportion of modern language teachers felt that they spent more time than they ought on problems of order and control and that they reported the highest numbers of troublesome pupils in their classes.

It appears then that the most common way secondary school teachers have of dealing with disruptive and inappropriate behaviour is to reprimand offending pupils rather than to encourage more appropriate classroom behaviour. A similar pattern is reflected in the systems schools employ to regulate pupils' behaviour. We were interested to know more about the rules and sanctions systems currently employed in secondary schools so we carried out a survey, using structured interviews with head teachers or their nominees, involving all of the secondary schools (24 in number) in a local education authority in the West Midlands. The structured interview schedule was designed to obtain information about the nature and form of the rules in each school and then to explore the sanction and reward systems devised to uphold them.

Most schools (21) had well-defined rule systems, usually written down, which were made available to all pupils (and their parents) when they began to attend the school. These rules usually formed part of an introductory booklet. In 12 schools the rules had been formulated within the last five years but in two, rules dated from 14 and 17 years previously and had not been reviewed since. This fact was a cause for concern to us in view of the rapid social changes which have taken place over this period and which are reflected in the changed relationships between teachers and their pupils.

Most schools used a hierarchy of sanctions to ensure that the pupils keep the rules which extend from telling off, lines or detention to writing to parents and involving them in the task of seeing that pupils conform. As a last resort, all schools had the sanctions of suspension or expulsion which involve outside authorities as well. There were very few examples of schools systematically providing rewards for pupils who behave well but a number of rewarding outcomes was provided in the academic and sporting spheres.

There is no doubt at all that teachers and the school environment generally, provide many consequences for the behaviour of pupils which are negative and, in a sense, punishing. For many youngsters, starting at the secondary school is a chance for a new beginning. They are starting with a clean slate as it were and for some this leads on to success. However, for some it does not. Some are overwhelmed by the complexity of the new organisation which confuses them and, unless they are given firm and kindly guidance in the early stages, they find themselves up against a system which is inflexible and which operates chiefly through sanctions and punishment of one sort or another. Our research referred to above underlines the fact that for a number of pupils, school as a social institution is providing few rewards. For some pupils, perhaps because their academic achievement up to this point has not been good and because their reading ability may not be very high, the classwork and, perhaps even more the homework, is altogether too hard. Some of the texts from which they are expected to work are simply beyond their reading comprehension. Teachers at the secondary level are not equipped to deal with large numbers of pupils who have not yet gained the basic skills of scholarship and these pupils find themselves left behind. After a while they give up altogether and form the residue of disaffection found in the upper age levels of many secondary schools.

Why are teachers so negative?

Why then do teachers and schools operate in such a negative fashion? One reason is that reprimands appear to work, and to work instantly. If a teacher shouts at a pupil to sit down or to stand up straight he or she will often respond at once. After a short while, however, the pupil may well be standing up or slouching once again but the immediate effect of the rebuke is rewarding for the teacher who will tend to repeat that sort of behaviour since it appeared to work. Secondly, we as teachers and parents are very good at spotting pupils behaving in ways that we object to, and feel that we have to respond at once. It has become a habit with us. Pupils, too, come to expect teachers to behave in this way towards them and if they do not do so they tend to brand such teachers as being soft. Generally, this is the way society is organised in that good behaviour is expected of us and goes unremarked whilst if we are caught doing something against the law we are punished. In the same way, teachers expect their pupils to behave well and tend to ignore them when behaving appropriately. It was, after all, the way that most teachers were treated when they were pupils themselves. On occasion, teachers may get frustrated and stressed and act without thinking. In any case, it is difficult to catch youngsters behaving well especially if they do not do it very often. Many teachers are not convinced that it is necessary to attend to appropriate behaviour. Furthermore, to do it well requires practice.

Disadvantages and side-effects of reprimands and punishment

These then may be some of the reasons why teachers tend to be negative towards their pupils. However, there are numerous disadvantages and practical problems which arise if the systems and methods employed by schools and teachers are essentially punitive and many unwanted side-effects are associated with them. First, prohibitive rules serve only to define what will not be tolerated but give no indication of alternative, appropriate behaviours. As mentioned above a rebuke or punishment may appear to work in the short term thus encouraging the adult to persevere with such a response. But for some pupils the attention they get when they offend is the only attention they ever get. When they do conform they are ignored and if attention is what they need (and which of us does not?) then pupil and teacher are locked into a vicious circle. Again, even when punishment does work its effect tends to diminish over time calling for more and more severe measures to control the situation. As we have said before, when this becomes more than pupils can bear they will seek to escape by lying or cheating or will avoid the situation altogether by staying away from the source of conflict by being absent from school.

Generally speaking, the use of negative and punishing sanctions for maintaining rules, or guidelines as some teachers prefer to call them, tends to precipitate conflict situations which are better avoided. In addition, such a system is providing a most unfortunate model for social behaviour. It is teaching, in effect, that might is right. It was for many of these reasons that corporal punishment in schools was abolished and this caused much anxiety to teachers who relied upon it. To use the argument that because society uses such a negative system we have to do the same in school is to miss the point entirely. Society's rule system is to *maintain* the behaviour of adults. School is the place for *teaching* acceptable behaviour to young people. In any case, the use of entirely punitive systems of control in society generally might well be questioned.

Most school rules, as in society at large, are framed in negative terms ("Thou shalt not") and sanctions are applied to those who disobey the eleventh commandment and allow themselves to be caught. A common characteristic of this system, which most teachers recognise, is that the sanctions apply to only a small minority of the pupil population. The same pupils' names tend to appear again and again in the punishment book often accompanied by the same teachers' names. This should cause us to question the effectiveness of the system.

Very few schools (only one in our survey discussed earlier) involved pupils (or junior staff, for that matter) in helping to frame the rules or even to approve them once decided upon and even fewer attempted to phrase their rules positively. Again, very few schools had any incentive system for rewarding pupils who keep to the rules and so conform well to the mores of the school society. Most schools had ways of rewarding pupils who achieve high standards in certain fields such as physical education, music and so on. However, apart from certificates for passing examinations which are long term and far beyond the reach of a large number of pupils, there is little by way of reward or encouragement for the majority and nothing to encourage appropriate behaviour in any of them. This is one of the positive factors that may emerge from the adoption of new assessment procedures which may accompany the new National Curriculum, but this remains to be seen.

Recognising appropriate behaviour

Our observational survey of teachers designed to measure the extent to which they use positive and negative responses to their pupils' work and behaviour also sampled the pupils' on-task behaviour. As already mentioned, it was found to be 80% on average. This is very high and yet some teachers were hardly ever referring to this high work rate, concentrating instead on the behaviour of those who were being a nuisance.

It is easy (only too easy, perhaps) to catch young people misbehaving in class. So far most of our attention has been directed towards misbehaviour and how we, as teachers, tend to react to it. Now we shall be turning to the other side of the coin, to appropriate behaviour and how we react to that. If we are trying to be more positive we need to be able to recognise appropriate behaviour easily and quickly. In order to do this we need to have definitions of clear, observable behaviours. Teachers or other observers must be able to identify the behaviours in question quickly and readily. If we are observing pupils in the classroom and wish to identify behaviours which could be classed as on-task we might be looking for pupils who are attending to (i.e. looking at) the teacher, pupils raising their hands and waiting to be called upon, pupils volunteering to respond by answering questions or by writing on the blackboard when asked, and so on. We referred to this earlier as pin-pointing, a very important skill for positive teachers.

What we want, as teachers, is for our pupils to improve both in their behavioural patterns and in their work. So what we have to look for is gradual improvement rather than excellence. Pupils who are not performing very well, whether academically or in terms of their behaviour, are not going to make enormous gains overnight. Spotting the very small increments they will make in the early stages is going to be difficult and will call for the most careful observation. This is why the development of observation skills and especially the precise pin-pointing of behaviours is regarded as being central to Positive Teaching.

An illustration may be appropriate here. At a school in the Inner London Education Authority the teachers decided after much discussion and consultation to give tokens to pupils for improvement in work or conduct. Each teacher had to find ten pupils every week who had improved in some way. To begin with they found it very difficult because they were not used to looking out for small increments of improved performance but after a week or two many of them found themselves dividing the tokens into smaller units because, with practice, they found more and more pupils they wanted to reward for improving. This study indicates that teachers can learn to observe and respond to improved work and behaviour on the part of their pupils and this is the issue that must concern us next.

At this stage it might be profitable for us to consider two linked questions. Why should we, as teachers, be concerned to recognise appropriate academic behaviour? The answer to this is clear. It is our job; to monitor and bring about improvement in their pupils' academic performance is what teachers are paid for. The second question is, perhaps, more controversial. Why should teachers be concerned with recognising and teaching social behaviour? Some teachers might argue that this is not their responsibility. There are even a few who seem to think that their sole concern is to dispense information about geography or French or whatever. Such teachers expect pupils to behave well and if they do not they blame the pupils themselves or their parents or suggest the sort of reasons we discussed as being unhelpful in Chapter One.

Most teachers would agree, however, that real teaching is about preparing pupils for life in a wider society and that teaching them to behave socially in appropriate ways is an important part of their remit. Good social behaviour, besides being an end in itself by oiling the wheels of social contact, is also an essential prerequisite for most kinds of learning within the group situation. Improved social skill enhances the opportunity for gaining academically for much is learned through social interactions of all kinds. More crudely, if pupils are being disruptive there is little chance for academic learning to take place however good the curriculum materials or the lesson preparation.

Responding to appropriate behaviour

Being skilful at observing what pupils are doing and what they are achieving is, however, only part of the game. Having observed appropriate behaviour or good learning we have to respond so as to increase the likelihood of that behaviour occurring again. In other words, we have to apply positive reinforcement. This raises two further issues. What is the pupil likely to find rewarding and how shall we deliver it? Most pupils will respond well to social reinforcement and this is relatively easy to dispense. Contrary to common belief secondary school pupils still respect and value the opinions of their teachers. When we put the question recently to a large number of pupils aged 11 - 16 about whom they were trying to please with regard to work and behaviour, the overwhelming majority said that it was the teacher rather than their peers. For most classes throughout the school more than 80% of boys and girls indicated that they regarded the opinions of their teachers as most important to them in matters both of work and conduct.

We all use social reinforcement. We all reward those around us at times for their behaviour towards us by the use of quite subtle signals of warmth and approval. We often smile at people in recognition or by way of thanks for something that they have done for us. We make encouraging remarks to people, we thank them for small services and we use all sorts of gestures to indicate approval. We can all learn to increase this behaviour and, by so doing, improve our relationships generally. It should be noted that it is not only what is said that matters. The tone of voice and general demeanour are also important. For example, it is very difficult to make a positive statement without, at the same time, smiling.

All of these comments and gestures except perhaps the smile have to be learned and the reponses to them are also the result of learning. Most of the pupils we meet in school have at least begun to respond to these social signals and with them we have a ready-made language of communication when we want to apply positive reinforcement. However, some of our pupils have not learned to respond so readily to social reinforcement and with them we have an additional problem, but it is still an educational problem and one which is our responsibility. We may have to use more extrinsic rewards initially, a point to which we return later.

In the last section we were considering behaviour which could be pin-pointed. The teacher might respond by praising pupils for engaging in such pin-pointed behaviours, ignoring minor misdemeanours. It is necessary to stress the need for a professional approach which uses discretion and involves a sense of timing. If you praise a group for working quietly for a time the result may well be that your comment will upset that quiet working pattern. It might be better, perhaps, to wait for a natural break before commenting. Giving a surprise treat occasionally as a consequence for acceptable behaviour like this has been found to be very effective.

With some pupils, teachers despair of finding anything they have to offer that their pupils will respond to. Nevertheless, we have to persevere because for every person living there are some things or events that they find rewarding. Above all, since everyone prefers some events or happenings to others, we can exploit Grandma's Law which says simply that outcomes which are enjoyed may be made dependent upon the completion of others which are less well-liked, with a view to increasing the latter. Grandma says to the young child, "You may have your ice cream when you have eaten all your first course" or, "You can go out to play when you have finished your chores". Similarly, the teacher can offer to allow the class free time, to start their homework, perhaps, or to allow individuals to choose a favourite activity once they have completed a set task.

Many teachers have been agreeably surprised when they find out that some pupils who appear to be very sophisticated do, in fact, respond well to some very simple outcomes that are arranged for them in response to improvement in work or behaviour. There are many ways of delivering rewards through Positive Teaching methods and some of these will be described in later chapters.

At secondary level and especially with older pupils it may sometimes be more appropriate to comment positively on academic achievements or improvements rather than social behaviour. You might comment positively on the social behaviour of the whole group but you would probably not find it expedient to do so with older pupils individually (except in private). In Chapter Four we shall be commenting further on pupils' preferences for praise and reward in secondary schools.

For positive reinforcement to be effective it must not only be appropriate but also sincere and is most effective if a variety of forms is used. A teacher may be using a lot of positive utterences but if all he or she ever says is "Good", "Well done" or "OK" then after a while these will lose their effect. If our positive social reinforcement is to be really effective then we have to employ a variety of gestures, statements and actions and suit these to persons and situations as appropriate. This is where our professional skill and our knowledge of our pupils comes into play. We are certainly not suggesting that praise should be scattered willy nilly like confetti regardless of behaviour or effort. In Positive Teaching we make praise and reward contingent upon appropriate work and behaviour. By contingent we mean that praise and reward should follow, and only follow, examples of appropriate behaviour. Positive reinforcement given non-contingently is likely to be counterproductive. For instance, if you congratulate a pupil on a piece of work and he or she knows it was achieved without any real effort, your comment will be wasted and your judgment will be called into question.

When we use social reinforcement we must always try to ensure that it is directed towards the behaviour rather than the person. We want it understood that it is the behaviour that is inappropriate or bad, for example, not the person and the same goes for good behaviour or satisfactory work. Of course, pupils will get satisfaction from the fact that their work or behaviour is worthy of praise but we try to avoid the implication that the person is good or bad *per se*. Our aim is to monitor pupils' behaviour and to respond to it appropriately, not to label them.

Let us consider two questions about positive reinforcement. First, why do you not have to prompt a teenager to ask for pocket money? The answer is obvious. Money is a reinforcer which, when you receive it, can make all sorts of other good things available to you. All human beings quickly learn to value money so it becomes a very general means of reinforcement for most people, most of the time.

The second question is, why do you have to keep reminding teenagers to wipe their shoes before coming into the house? Obviously wiping your feet has no pay-off. Any mess made is cleaned up by someone else. When do they learn? It is amazing what a difference it makes to this sort of behaviour when youngsters acquire a place of their own. Then they have to clean up the mess they make or live in squalor (and some, of course, initially do just that!). When they have to find the money to replace worn out or dirty furnishings their response to the importance of simple habits which make things last longer or look better changes because, once again, there is a clear pay-off.

Some social behaviours are followed by powerful positive rein-forcers (such as money) although most (like wiping your feet) are not. Few academic skills are associated with immediately reward-ing outcomes. Part of the task of teachers (and parents), as educators, is to provide young people with extrinsic positive rein-forcement until the time when the behaviour will be maintained by intrinsic reinforcement. If you read this book and find it satisfying a need so that you feel that you have learned something from it and can now begin to do your job with greater confidence, then nobody will need to praise you for reading it. The reward is intrinsic, built into the task itself. The same applies to a recipe that you manage to apply with success.

Those of our pupils who succeed in their academic work and in their social and sporting life in school will be receiving a great deal of intrinsic satisfaction from all these activities. But what about those who are less successful? They are getting few rewards and we have to structure a situation in which we provide extrinsic reward systems for them until they, too, begin to enjoy the intrinsic rewards which come from being successful and accepted by those around them. For some, starting a long way back in the race, this is going to be a lengthy process but it is all part of our remit as teachers. Positive teachers do not go in for labelling this or that pupil as remedial or hyperactive and then assume that nothing can be done. They do not indulge in such explanatory fictions but prefer, instead, to observe carefully, find some positive elements in the pupil's behaviour and to work to increase those. As soon as it can be arranged for the pupil to receive some reward for behaviour which is profitable for him or her, for the other pupils or the teacher we are on the way to improvement. One of the chief difficulties is to find something that is likely to be rewarding for pupils who have found very few rewards in the system so far. One event to which most of them will respond favourably is the under-standing and acceptance that somebody is interested in their problem and ready to offer practical help. The various ways in which this can be achieved will be discussed more fully in Chapters Four and Five.

Nothing that has been written so far is meant to give the impression that it is easy to be a positive teacher. If the effects of the approach are to be maximised then we need to use our imagination, initiative and resourcefulness to the full. Positive Teaching is no panacea. It is not to be thought of as an ointment that can be rubbed on and left to do the job. To achieve effective classroom management by means of Positive Teaching teachers have to monitor their own behaviour. In order to improve our skill in observing and responding to pupils we have to practise.

We need to find times when we are teaching, and it must be admitted that teaching is a task which takes almost all of our energy and concentration, when we can observe our pupils and ourselves. For this we need a schedule of some kind on which we have written a clear definition of what we are looking for and some simple system for recording events. Alternatively, a tally counter, a mechanical device which records numbers successively as it is pressed, may be found useful. These can be bought at some stationers but are, unfortunately, rather expensive. Some hand calculators can be programmed to do the same thing. Another way is to arrange with a colleague to observe you in action and then to reciprocate. This method is likely to give you an indication of how good you are at using positive and negative responding effectively. We will return to this issue in Chapter Four. Descriptions of simple observation schedules and how teachers can monitor their own behaviour may be found in our earlier book, *Positive Teaching: the behavioural approach.*

Our research shows that teachers can be positive, encouraging and supportive of pupils' academic efforts but when it comes to their classroom behaviour the emphasis appears to be almost overwhelmingly negative. The continual litany of reprimands we hear on entering some secondary classes is almost always an attempt to deal with disruptive classroom behaviours. The focus is on detecting and dealing with inappropriate behaviour rather than recognising and rewarding appropriate behaviour. Very rarely are attempts made to encourage more appropriate forms of classroom behaviour. Similarly, the systems which schools develop for maintaining discipline are structured so as to punish transgressions rather than to encourage more responsible behaviour. Teachers and schools attempting to apply Positive Teaching techniques will have to engineer changes in systems and practices. The means for bringing about changes in pupils' behaviour and their academic standards are available. What teachers have to decide is whether it is worth the effort.

Further reading

A more detailed account of the principles and procedures of Positive Teaching is given in our earlier work:

Wheldall, K. and Merrett, F. (1984). *Positive Teaching: the behavioural approach.* London: Allen & Unwin, reprinted 1989 by Positive Products, Birmingham.

The application of Positive Teaching methods to encourage academic learning is detailed in:

Wheldall, K. and Glynn, T. (1989). *Effective Classroom Learning: a behavioural interactionist approach to teaching.* Oxford: Basil Blackwell.

Our observational study of secondary school teachers' use of praise and reprimands is reported fully in:

Wheldall, K., Houghton, S. and Merrett, F. (1989). Natural rates of teacher approval and disapproval in British secondary school classrooms. *British Journal of Educational Psychology, 59,* 38-48.

Our study of secondary school rule systems is fully reported in:

Merrett, F., Wilkins, J., Houghton, S. and Wheldall, K. (1988). Rules, sanctions and rewards in secondary schools. *Educational Studies, 14,* 139-149.

Chapter Three
SETTING THE CLASSROOM CONTEXT

Most teachers will have noticed how the behaviour of a class varies depending on who is teaching them, where they are being taught or even who has been teaching them in the previous lesson. This is particularly noticeable in secondary schools where pupils may be taught by several different teachers in different rooms during the course of the day. Being with a certain teacher or even in that teacher's room may be the cue for unruly behaviour because pupils have learned that they can get away with such behaviour with that particular teacher in that situation. With another teacher and in a different room few of the same group of children would dare even to breathe too loudly having expectations of the second teacher's likely response to any such behaviour, however harmless. Similarly, academic lessons, held by necessity in the craft design technology or art room may lead to more disruptive behaviour than when held in a regular classroom. Being in the art room has become associated with a different form of behaviour, involving more movement around the room perhaps.

As we have said, it is not sufficient to attempt to explain learning simply in terms of behaviours and reinforcers as we have done so far. As well as considering what happens after a behaviour occurs (the consequence) we should also consider what happened just before the behaviour occurred and the context in which it occurred (the antecedents). As already mentioned in Chapter One, antecedent events also have great power to influence behaviour.

Antecedents can serve to prompt certain behaviours. Consider the situation when a teacher leaves the room and the class is left alone. For some classes this may have become a cue for noisy, disruptive behaviour since there is no-one present to reprimand the pupils. When the teacher returns, the noisy disruptive behaviour will cease. We can see here how specific antecedent conditions influence particular behaviours in association with certain consequences.

Let us take another example which highlights how this might occur. The teacher asks Jenny a question in class (antecedent), Jenny gives a silly answer (behaviour) and her classmates laugh (consequence). Since this laughter is probably rewarding for her we may expect Jenny to produce silly answers on similar occasions subsequently. She will be less likely to do so, however, when her classmates are not there. The presence of classroom peers has become a cue for her inappropriate behaviour. This example underlines the need to consider the context in which behaviours occur and demonstrates how some antecedents develop their power to influence behaviour.

Within the classroom environment it is known that a wide range of antecedent events will influence behaviour and they do this in at least two basic ways. First, there are those antecedent conditions which provide constraints or opportunities for behaviour. We are thinking here of factors such as seating arrangements or the presence or absence of particular materials or curriculum aids or of other people. Secondly, there are antecedent conditions which have acquired power over certain behaviours by association with rewarding or punishing circumstances, as we have shown above. Antecedents encompass a variety of features of the environment which may influence pupils' behaviour. These features range from specific actions by a teacher or another pupil to more global aspects of the environment such as heating and lighting levels, the arrangement of furniture and materials and the management of classroom seating.

This key principle of Positive Teaching, that children's behaviour can be greatly influenced by antecedent contextual factors, appears to be little appreciated and greatly under-utilized in classroom teaching. Positive teachers should identify which particular antecedents in their classrooms have clear effects on children's learning. They can then work to manipulate some of these, for most are under their direct control, to bring about changes in the climate of the classroom. When teachers make effective use of antecedent events to encourage appropriate behaviour they have more time to spend on teaching and instruction.

The importance of curriculum issues

Before embarking upon discussion of the importance of the various key antecedents in more detail it is necessary to establish one fact of vital importance about the learning/teaching situation. The curriculum materials with which the teacher seeks to engage the attention of his or her pupils must be appropriate. They must be appropriate in terms of what the pupils know already and the skills they have at their disposal. They must relate to the curriculum elements about to be tackled and, above all, they must present a challenge and be of interest to the pupils. We have to accept that not all learning can be of compelling interest and fascination all of the time. Mastery of some skills, techniques and procedures calls for prolonged practice and some of this practice can be quite boring and, for the time being, apparently fruitless. But life and work are like that and youngsters have to learn to be tolerant of some learning and work processes, elements of which are not immediately exciting.

Nevertheless, it is possible to leaven the lump and most of what pupils do in school should appeal, should be exciting and should have obvious value for them, even if not in the immediate future. If the curriculum they are led to follow is without some excitement, some challenge, some enjoyment and if it does not aim eventually at the pupils' ultimate and lasting good, it cannot be called educational and has no place in the school or the classroom. Her Majesty's Inspectorate have called attention more than once to the importance of matching the content of the curriculum to the needs of pupils. If we are serious about equality of opportunity we must recognise the need for a curriculum appropriate for all our pupils whatever their cultural or social background. There is no need to labour this point further here, but it is fundamental to all that follows.

What we are not endorsing is that old cliché, so well-loved by some college lecturers, that provided you have prepared your lesson properly you will have no discipline problems. Most teachers will know from bitter experience that some classes or pupils will be troublesome regardless of the amount of time, creativity and energy spent in preparing exciting and relevant lessons. On the other hand, it is only fair to add that some pupil misbehaviour may be perceived as a legitimate protest against tedious lessons on topics of little relevance presented in a pedestrian and boring manner.

The following small-scale study illustrates the importance of curriculum materials, in this case choice of reading materials, to classroom behaviour. The study was carried out in a comprehensive school in the West Midlands where a group of 23 first year pupils was observed daily during English lessons. Typically the pupils spent the first half of each lesson reading from their set book, *The Silver Sword,* and the second half producing a written comment on what they had read. Initial observations of the class for ten 30-minute lessons indicated an average on-task level of around 67%. For the next five lessons pupils were asked to bring in a reading book of their own choice from home or from the library and to use that as a basis for their class work. The average on-task level rose immediately to around 87%. For the final week of the study the class reader once again became the focus of the class comprehension exercise. The average on-task level fell back to about 67%. Clearly, *The Silver Sword* was, for these pupils, an inappropriate stimulus for recreational reading and report writing.

Arranging the classroom

We now turn to a consideration of the ecology of the classroom. It has been demonstrated quite clearly that the conditions under which people work affects their output. If they are cold, hungry, unduly worried or stressed they cannot perform up to their usual standard. Likewise, if pupils cannot hear what the teacher is saying because he or she is too far away or is speaking too softly or with an unfamiliar accent they will soon lose the sense of what is going on and will cease to attend. Sometimes pupils are hindered in following the interaction because they cannot see clearly what is being demonstrated on the blackboard or the bench. All of these are very obvious reasons for pupils' difficulties and most of them are under the direct and easy control of the teacher. However, the teacher must be aware of them, be vigilant to notice them and respond to remove them whenever possible. Some teachers, especially those who are new to the profession, are so concerned with other matters of presentation or procedure that they are not aware of such problems and fail to see how they can be avoided.

Another source of problems is movement in the classroom. Sometimes it is necessary and desirable for pupils to move about in the classroom in order to gain access to equipment, to refer to charts, dictionaries or other resource materials. Therefore, it must be made possible for them to do so easily and efficiently without disturbing others. In addition, they have to know where the materials they need are to be found, what the procedures are for gaining permission to use them (if this is thought to be necessary) and they have to have access to proper routeways so they have unhindered passage. All of this calls for careful planning in the arrangement of furniture and of the storage facilities for the convenience of the group. In addition, it underlines the need for agreed procedures for giving out and collecting in (and checking) equipment. Routines for such basic administrative procedures are absolutely essential for a well-run classroom and experienced, successful teachers know that they can reduce much of the daily stress.

Teachers' control of seating arrangements is another area which needs attention in some classrooms. In some situations it is a good idea to allow pupils to choose where they sit. In others it can be a recipe for disaster. There is no doubt at all that by manipulating seating arrangements changes can be brought about in the behaviour of pupils. Most teachers will be aware that in some classes a certain group of pupils will seek seats (usually at the back of the room) in order to carry on certain ploys which they, the teachers, find annoying or disruptive to the rest of the class. By insisting that such pupils occupy seats designated by themselves, teachers may be able to control the situation. Again, pupils who are constantly off-task or interfering with the work of others around them can often be brought into line by moving them to sit nearer the teacher or away from peers who are reinforcing their behaviour with attention.

These examples are anecdotal but more formal experiments have been carried out to show that such strategies are based upon sound principles. We have been able to show that simple manipulation of seating arrangements between pupils sitting in rows or around tables in top junior classes can bring about quite large changes in the pupils' on-task behaviour. For individual seat-work, where pupils are required to get on with academic work independently and without interruption (a common requirement), sitting in rows has been shown to be preferable to sitting around tables. Pupils spend 15% to 20% more time getting on with the work that has been set and they produce more work, generally of a better standard. Clearly, pupils will interact more in the manifestly social context which is provided by seating around tables. Tables seating facilitates the exchange of ideas and that is why we arrange seating in this way for dinner parties, committee meetings and so on. Similarly, when we want pupils to work collaboratively or to discuss issues in a group then tables seating is ideal. The important thing is to match the seating arrangements to the task in hand.

The effects of changed seating arrangements have also been demonstrated with secondary aged classes as the following studies show. The first study was carried out with a group of 12 below-average ability third-year students in a small comprehensive school. To begin with the classroom was arranged so that the (two-seater) tables were arranged together in pairs, i.e. with four pupils sitting facing each other. Observations carried out over six lessons showed that on-task behaviour averaged 52%. The tables were then arranged in rows so that no pupil faced another. On-task behaviour rose to around 84%. When the original seating was resumed the average level of on-task behaviour fell back to about 52% but rose again to 91% when rows were reintroduced. During the fourth phase the pupils were also given the opportunity to record the number of questions they were able to complete and this may have helped to boost the on-task level for this phase. This study shows clearly that seating arrangements are as important in the secondary as in the primary school.

An example of changing antecedents with a group of older pupils is provided by another study, carried out in a college of further education. The group comprised 11 boys and girls, all 16 years of age and of rather low academic ability enrolled in a YTS scheme in motor vehicle stores handling. Preliminary observations over five lessons showed that on-task behaviour averaged 64%. The chairs and tables had been arranged in three rows and it was obvious that the on-task behaviour of the pupils in the back row was much lower than that of the front row. It was decided to change the setting by removing all surplus chairs and tables and arranging the necessary furniture in a single line semi-circle facing the chalk board. The lecturer was asked to stand in front of, rather than behind, his bench so as to be closer to the group for better interaction to take place. Overall, average on-task behaviour rose to 75%. Again, the change in seating arrangements brought about a positive change in behaviour.

The last study was carried out in a large comprehensive school in the West Midlands with a below-average third year class of 27 boys and girls, generally regarded by staff as troublesome. Classroom observations were completed during history lessons taught by a male graduate of five years' experience. The class was normally seated in rows of same-sex pairs. It was observed that as they could choose where they sat, boys chose to sit next to boys whilst girls typically chose to sit next to girls. They were first observed on three separate occasions over a two-week period before the intervention began. During the two-week intervention phase pupils were instructed not to sit next to a member of the same sex and they were again observed on three occasions. In the third phase (again of two weeks) pupils were allowed to resume same-sex seating and were observed on three more occasions.

During each observation lesson every pupil was observed in random order at least twice for thirty seconds. The observer noted on an observation schedule whether or not that individual had been on-task. On-task behaviour was defined as paying attention to the relevant materials or to the teacher when he was speaking, carrying out the teacher's instructions and staying in-seat. Percentage on-task estimates were calculated for each individual pupil and for the whole class.

Average on-task behaviour for the class during the customary (same-sex) seating was 76% but this rose to 91% during the mixed-sex seating intervention. When same-sex seating was resumed average on-task behaviour fell back to 83%. These results show that both boys and girls spent more time attending to their work when seated next to a member of the opposite sex than when seated next to a person of the same sex. Subsequent discussion with the pupils revealed that, in general, they felt that they concentrated on their work less when seated next to (same-sex) friends and that they had worked harder during the intervention phase. This study, once again, clearly demonstrates the influence of ecological factors such as seating arrangements on classroom behaviour.

We are not necessarily advocating this type of seating arrangement, although there will be times when it could be used to good effect, to establish some measure of control with an unruly class, for example. What we would emphasise is the importance of matching the seating arrangements to the task in hand. More generally, positive teachers seek to optimise the classroom environment so as to encourage appropriate behaviour and effective learning.

Ensuring the smooth flow of the lesson

Once we have made sure that the subject matter is appropriate for the pupils and that the ecological factors in the classroom setting are right it is then important to ensure that the lesson proceeds smoothly. When a group of pupils is well-organised so that each knows what has to be done and in what order, there is less danger that things will get out of hand. Some of the confusion and disruption we observe in classrooms stems from the fact that some of the pupils cannot cope for one reason or another or that they have completed their work quickly and do not know what else to occupy themselves with.

First and foremost, teachers must ensure that their pupils understand clearly the nature of the task that has been set. If instructions are given verbally the teacher must be sure that all have heard them clearly and understand. In order to find out if this is the case the teacher can ask one of the pupils to recount the instructions. Once a teacher gets to know his or her students it is easy to pick pupils who are less likely to attend to instructions. Once we feel sure that such pupils have got the full message we can have confidence that most of the others will also. Generally speaking, it is best if teachers refrain from repeating their instructions as this teaches pupils that they do not have to listen the first time instructions are given out since they will shortly be repeated. It is always better to have another student repeat instructions for the rest, if this proves to be necessary.

Once instructions have been given they have to be remembered and another opportunity for misunderstanding or interruption of the learning process can occur when pupils, having made a good start, then fail to recall what they have to do next. One way of overcoming this problem is to divide the process into small sections and to give directions for each separately as they are completed. This can give rise to other problems, however, as all will not proceed at the same pace, but if the teacher is moving round the group in order to keep an eye on the progress being made, it can be a useful device. If the learning process or the sequence of tasks is complicated it is probably best if the instructions are given in written form, perhaps on a blackboard or flipchart, so that reference to this can be made at any juncture for additional guidance. This is where worksheets come into their own. Where instructions are complicated, or if pupils are not good readers, they probably need to be taken through the script before being asked to make a start. In these cases diagrams, especially flow diagrams, may be a useful aid.

It will probably be helpful if details of equipment or other necessary materials are also listed on worksheets. It was mentioned above that procedures for obtaining equipment are an important factor in classroom management. Failure on the part of the pupils to bring the necessary equipment is a frequent cause of interruption to the smooth flow of a lesson. If teachers can arrange for pupils to be warned, in advance, of any extra equipment they will need for certain lessons this is less likely to happen. Teachers should always ensure that equipment commonly needed for work in their subject is routinely available. This may sound obvious and as though we are trying to teach grandmothers to suck eggs but, as the Elton Report makes clear, it is surprising how often such elementary procedures are not observed.

If the subject matter to be taught involves equipment that is not used every day the teacher will do well to think through carefully the method by which it is to be made available. Perhaps it is best if the material is placed ready for use before the lesson begins. In some circumstances, however, this can be counter-productive. If prior explanation is necessary then the presence of new or unfamiliar equipment within easy reach may be difficult for some pupils to resist and they may begin to play with it. In such cases it is necessary to decide at which point the introduction of the equipment is going to be most useful and to consider carefully the best method of distribution. These issues are not trivial in terms of classroom management and can make the difference between the success and failure of otherwise carefully prepared lessons. In some subjects frequent changes of classroom seating are necessary whilst in others pupils frequently need to have access to pieces of equipment kept in the room as, for example, in laboratories, workshops or craft rooms. In such cases it is well worthwhile to spend time at the beginning of the school year practising the correct procedures for altering the seating arrangements or for obtaining equipment.

In a well-ordered classroom it is necessary also to have routines for the pupils to follow when they need help. Most teachers will ask their pupils to raise their hands if they want to contribute to discussion or need help and this works well enough in most instances. Nevertheless, there are drawbacks to this procedure because it means that when several pupils are seeking help at the same time, some may be kept waiting for quite long periods with nothing to do. As mentioned above, delays which cause interruption to the smooth flow of the lesson are prone to lead to problems in classroom management and should be avoided if at all possible. Another common device is to invite pupils who have problems to come to the teacher sitting at his or her desk. This, too, can work well but unless care is taken to prevent it, may lead to long queues building up. Standing in a queue provides opportunities for all sorts of misbehaviour.

It will readily be seen that having too many pupils not knowing what to do next, or how to proceed, is closely linked to the discussion earlier about the appropriateness of the task. Nevertheless, there will be occasions when many of the pupils are having difficulty. On such occasions it will often be found that they share a common problem or that there is a common misunderstanding. In such cases it will be necessary to stop the lesson briefly and to explain a way around the problem for the whole or part of the class. In lessons where there are several procedures or several sections to be attempted it is possible to accustom pupils to register the fact that they need help and then to turn to another section they can cope with, whilst they are waiting for the teacher to attend to them.

It will be appreciated that much of the discussion so far in this section has been to ensure that the lesson, once begun, should flow smoothly giving little opportunity for undesirable or disruptive behaviour. Pupils who have plenty to occupy their attention, work which they find absorbing and which is within their capacities, will usually be prepared to get on with it and will have little time or opportunity for upsetting the rest of the group.

There is one other situation which can give rise to problems of classroom management and that is when pupils finish the work which has been set and do not know what to do next. Once again, this occurrence can be the result of poor planning or of poor instruction about what has to be done. In well-ordered classrooms the teacher will always be aware of the necessity for pupils to have work to do when for one reason or another they have completed the task or tasks which have been set for the day or the period. This is made easier where, as in most secondary schools, homework is part of the school routine. The opportunity to get on with homework, which normally encroaches upon pupils' private time, is always welcome and allows the teacher to benefit from the operation of Grandma's Law as explained in Chapter Two. In other words, a task which is more acceptable is made contingent upon first completing one which is less agreeable.

A study which demonstrates the importance of pupils having additional or alternative tasks was carried out in a large comprehensive school in a deprived, urban area and involved a difficult class of 25 low-ability 14 year-olds. All of their teachers admitted to having difficulties with this class. The headmaster, who taught remedial mathematics to this class for five lessons per week, volunteered to take part in our study. He was an impressive teacher, who used relatively high rates of praise, but our initial observations showed that the pupils were on-task (getting on with their set work) for only about 55% of the time, compared with the average for secondary classes of 80%. Many of the students were often off-task because they had finished the set work and did not know what to do next. Others had not finished but were being disturbed by those who had. Our first suggestion was for more maths problems to be provided for the quicker pupils to get on with while the slower ones caught up. The headteacher followed this advice and, as a result, on-task behaviour immediately rose to around 70%. This study demonstrates the power of antecedents, such as changing the work demands, on classroom behaviour. We subsequently improved the behaviour of this class still further using other strategies as we shall describe in Chapter Five.

Setting effective classroom rules

Another major set of antecedents which influence classroom behaviour are classroom rules. All social groups have rules and school classes are no exception to this. In many social situations the rules are implicit and we learn to abide by and accept these implied rules because to do so oils the wheels of social contact. If we voluntarily join a group of other people for some common purpose then we have an incentive for learning their rules. But school classes are artificial groupings where the members are arbitrarily selected for a particular purpose, that of instruction and learning together. The rules are often implicit or unclear and are generally imposed by teachers. Pupils have to learn to accommodate to them as far as they are able but this calls for interpretation on their part. This can result in unfortunate outcomes for some pupils. They may adopt strategies which seem to them to conform to what they believe the teacher expects but which are, in fact, unproductive for learning.

From a Positive Teaching perspective we would suggest that rules are of great importance in schools and in classes and that they should be made explicit. Positive teachers will arrive at a set of rules not by imposing them but through negotiation with their pupils. Even quite young children are capable of understanding how a set of reasonable rules can make the classroom climate more acceptable and how they can make life easier and more pleasant for all. If pupils are asked to suggest rules they will probably come up with some very negative suggestions at first, to be supported by equally negative sanctions. This is not what we have in mind, however. We have to accept their suggestions and then encourage the pupils to translate them into a more positive form.

There are three key criteria for effective classroom rules. First, we believe that classroom rules should be positively phrased specifying appropriate behaviour rather than prohibiting inappropriate behaviour. Secondly, they should be specific and objective so that the situation and the behaviour are clearly defined, allowing both teacher and pupils to know when the rules are being kept. Finally, classroom rules should be practical. There is no point in asking for the impossible and we find that the inclusion of the word *try* in rules makes them more acceptable and practicable.

If a teacher says that there is to be no talking then he or she has to be alert to catch the first pupil to break the rule and do something about it otherwise his or her authority will be under threat. There is a danger that pupils may learn that this teacher makes rule statements but does not enforce them. On the other hand if the teacher negotiates rules such as, "We try to work quietly" then he or she can concentrate on appropriate behaviour and pay attention to pupils who are keeping the rules. Positive rules help us to avoid conflict.

Some people might argue that because the rules of society are framed in the form of "Thou shalt not" and are supported by sanctions of one sort or another, schools should maintain the same structure. However, it must be appreciated that society's rules are meant to maintain the behaviour of adults whereas in school we have a different objective, namely the teaching of new behaviours to a fresh generation and this confronts us with quite different problems. The positive teacher then will seek to negotiate through discussion with his or her pupils a set of rules which are phrased positively, which are seen to be reasonable and which pupils believe they can keep. These rules should be few in number (not more than three or four) and should be written down. In the case of younger pupils they may be written on a notice and displayed prominently but with older pupils it may be better if they write them in their notebooks.

When pupils are working with a set of imposed and negative rules it is usual for those in control to call attention to the rules when they have been broken. A child will be punished and reminded at the same time that he or she has broken a stated rule. When positive rules are negotiated we write them down so that they may be referred to at suitable times (the beginning of the week, say) to remind those who have agreed to them what we are striving to do for the comfort and convenience of all. Because their number is few they do not have to remain the same for ever. In fact, once pupils have become accustomed to keeping a rule, that rule may be dropped and another can take its place. For instance, let us assume that one of the original rules was to raise your hand and wait to be asked if you want to answer a question. After a while this may become second nature to the members of the group and may be replaced by a rule dealing with more polite ways of interacting with one's neighbours. As we have said, it has been found that to use the word *try* in defining the rules is useful because one can still be congratulated for trying even when one has not succeeded. We will return to the important issue of classroom rules in Chapter Five.

So far what has been discussed has related to the classroom but in secondary schools pupils are subject also to another rule system which is general to the school. It is important that this, too, should be positive in its outlook but this state of affairs can only be brought about by concerted action of the whole staff. In Chapter Two we discussed our research on how most school rules comprise sanction systems imposed by senior management. It is self-evident that if people feel that they have had some say in what the rules are to be they will be better motivated to keep them. Ideally, this should apply to pupils in school also. If they are to learn how a rule system (designed to teach acceptable behaviour and democratically arrived at) is to work, what better model could they have than that of their own school?

Further reading

One of the studies on classroom seating arrangements is reported in:

Merrett, F. and Wheldall, K. (1988). Case studies in Positive Teaching II: more examples showing behavioural strategies in action at the secondary level. *Behavioural Approaches with Children, 12,* 25-35.

A chapter detailing our research on classroom seating arrangements is included in:

Wheldall, K. and Glynn, T. (1989). *Effective Classroom Learning: a behavioural interactionist approach to teaching.* Oxford: Basil Blackwell.

Our study on the effect of setting additional work is reported in:

Wheldall, K. and Merrett, F. (1985). Reducing troublesome class-room behaviour in the secondary school: the behavioural approach. *Maladjustment and Therapeutic Education, 3,* 37-46.

Chapter Four
ENHANCING PRAISE AND REPRIMANDS

In his famous essay *On Education*, the seventeenth-century philosopher, John Locke wrote, "Esteem and disgrace are, of all others, the most powerful incentives to the mind, when once it is brought to relish them". Locke regarded the achievement of this as "the great secret of education". He continued,

> Children (earlier perhaps than we think) are very sensible of praise and commendation. They find a pleasure in being esteemed and valued, especially by their parents, and those whom they depend on.

Locke's comments on praise, first aired over 300 years ago, may sound painfully obvious to many teachers but it is our contention that the lesson has still to be learned.

Most teachers would agree that to use encouragement and approval is more effective than to rely upon negative procedures with their pupils. A key principle of Positive Teaching is finding out what pupils will respond to or go for. This will vary from person to person, from situation to situation and from time to time, but not all that much. For most people most of the time we can be fairly sure what things will be positively reinforcing. Giving people things to eat and drink or things to wear are reinforcing. We respond to such items naturally because they are, in the last resort, necessary for life. Likewise, adults and most children respond to attention and to social signals like gestures and statements of approval. Such social signals, except perhaps smiling, which is a very powerful one, have had to be learned. Such social gestures become reinforcing through being associated with other reinforcers, like the natural ones mentioned above, on many occasions from early on in life.

Some reinforcers, of which money is the best example, owe their reinforcing power to the fact that they give free access to other things which are in themselves reinforcing. Such reinforcers are called tokens and their great advantage is that they make it possible to reinforce immediately and in situations where the use of primary reinforcement would be difficult. This situation frequently obtains in schools and hence marks, stars and points are often used as tokens. It is important to realise that they are only effective when their power is understood and valued by all those involved. To begin with, therefore, they must be clearly linked with established reinforcers such as preferred activities or special treats of some sort or other.

In order to use reinforcement effectively we have to identify what is positively reinforcing for the pupil(s) in a given situation and then learn to use this knowledge to shape up desired behaviours whether social or academic. As stated above, we can only find out what is reinforcing to an individual, a group or a class by trying it out to see if it works but we can get some good ideas as to what is likely to be reinforcing by:

1. observing pupils when they have freedom of choice, or

2. by asking them what they like to do best.

Anything or any activity which a pupil enjoys and over which we have control in school can be used as a reinforcer. Extra time to carry on some activity, to listen to records, to play games, to go out to break or to go home early, to help in the classroom, or to use certain pieces of apparatus or just to be given a free choice of occupation have all been used successfully as positive reinforcers with adolescents. Many of these activities can be educational in themselves. If we can make their availability dependent upon some clear criteria for behaviour over a certain period or in a certain situation then we shall begin to exert influence over that behaviour. For example, a few minutes extra on a favoured activity in P.E. can be made dependent upon an agreed level of quietness and/or speed in the changing room.

What do secondary pupils regard as effective rewards and punishments?

A reservation which some secondary teachers may, initially, have about the behavioural approach to teaching is that it can be difficult to determine effective rewards with troublesome or poorly motivated secondary aged pupils. The disenchanted, potentially troublesome, teenage pupil is less likely to find the traditional privilege of feeding the guinea pig rewarding. So it is reasonable to ask, "What do secondary aged pupils find rewarding?" To this end, we carried out two consumer surveys on this topic. A simple questionnaire was designed in which pupils were asked to select their answers to a series of questions from a number of alternatives. Despite the fact that the language was purposely kept very simple, each item and the list of answers was read aloud as pupils worked through the sheet. This was done because it was known that some students would have difficulty in reading the text with meaning and to ensure that no invidious distinctions should be made.

In our first study the attitudes and opinions of nearly 400 12-16 year-olds attending two comprehensive schools in the West Midlands were surveyed. The Praise and Rewards Attitude Questionnaire was employed to enquire into pupils' preferences for various types of reward for both academic work and classroom behaviour. It was found that most of the pupils who took part did perceive rewards and praise as appropriate outcomes for both, although older pupils generally regarded them as more appropriate for academic behaviour alone. The results also showed that when offered a choice of six alternative rewards (sweets, free time, no reward, praise, points or a positive letter home), free time and a positive letter home were the most highly regarded. Free time was, perhaps, to be expected as an acceptable reward. It is relatively easy to arrange and has often been shown to be effective. A positive letter home was much less predictable and is hardly ever employed in secondary schools. A letter home is normally used to convey disapproval of social or academic behaviour.

A subsequent study replicated and extended these findings by using a very similar instrument to ask, in addition, what punishments and sanctions secondary pupils considered to be effective in bringing about behaviour change, this time with nearly 900 pupils. Once again, free time and a letter home were regarded as effective rewards for both academic work and classroom behaviour whilst the most effective punishments were perceived to be a letter home complaining about some aspect of work or behaviour and being put on report. The least effective punishments, according to all pupils, were being sent out and being told off. The pupils involved were also asked about their views on the opinions of their teachers and of their peers about matters of discipline and work. Perhaps surprisingly, the vast majority of pupils (over 80%) claimed to value their teachers' opinions about their work and their conduct more highly than that of their peers.

There appears to be a mismatch between the punishments and sanctions most used by teachers (like telling off and sending out) and those regarded as effective by their pupils. On the other hand some actions (both punishments and rewards) which are regarded as effective by pupils are seldom, if ever, used by teachers. An example of this is the positive letter home which, when used, has been found to be very effective. It would appear that further research is needed in this area if teachers' actions are to be more effective. In addition to teachers' and pupils' opinions we need to know much more about the incidence of praise and rewarding strategies, about how effective each is found to be and with which groups they will work and what efforts have been made to improve their effectiveness. Common sense would suggest that most of the punishments which uphold the rule systems of schools fall upon the very few but have little effect.

Making reprimands more effective

Some teachers use reprimands quite frequently but not very effectively. We can tell that this is so because they are using them all the time. If their reprimands were effective in punishing a behaviour they are directed towards, that behaviour would be choked off and the reprimands would decrease accordingly. For example, a teacher may observe that one pupil is disturbing others in the class by his behaviour. He is not getting on with his own work and instead is preventing others from making progress with theirs. The teacher is not quite sure what to do but decides that he or she has to intervene in some way. The teacher says, "Charlie, stop messing about and get on with your work or I'll come over there and sort you out". Unless this does have the intended effect and thereby stops Charlie misbehaving it will probably mean that the next time the teacher observes the same sort of event he or she will either ignore it, in the hope that it will cease, or be forced into some more serious confrontation.

Positive teachers do not ignore situations like these nor does positive teaching imply that reprimands should never be used. Reprimands have a very real place in the repertoire of positive teachers but they will prove to be most effective when they occur infrequently in a climate that is predominantly positive. In order to make reprimands effective they should be delivered from close quarters, not shouted across the room for everyone to hear. Reducing the personal distance allows the teacher to speak in a quiet but firm tone to make it perfectly clear that he or she is displeased with the behaviour that has been observed and does not intend that it shall continue. It is best if teachers can, at the same time, remain quite calm and show that they do not feel threatened by the situation. It may, occasionally, be necessary to spell out some consequence or sanction which will follow if the unwanted behaviour does not cease and this, too, is in keeping with the positive approach. Of course, the promised punishment or sanction must be reasonable and in accord with the common policy of the school and it must be carried out exactly as promised or the teacher's credibility and status will suffer. It is worth repeating, however, that reprimands are most effective when used sparingly in a generally positive teaching context.

This is clearly illustrated by our research study which compared two behaviour management procedures in four secondary school classes. The teachers, three men and one woman, had an average of 13 years' teaching experience and each admitted that the behaviour of their classes could be better. Observation of their classroom behaviour gathered over a period of three weeks revealed that two of the teachers used very high rates of loud (public) reprimands and low rates of praise with their second and third year classes.

These two teachers were then shown a video sequence taken from the BATSAC course (see Chapter Five) demonstrating how to give effective reprimands. They were asked to try to copy the model seen giving reprimands on the video recording. This requires the teacher to move close to the pupil, to engage eye contact and to state briefly but firmly exactly what is being disapproved of. Above all, the reprimands were to be given quietly as a private exchange between the two. They were also asked to try to reduce their use of reprimands to ten or fewer in each double lesson of 70 minutes. In order to help them to achieve this, both teachers were given hand tally-counters so that they could readily count the number of reprimands they gave. Subsequent observation showed that they were both able to meet their targets. As a result the average levels of pupil on-task behaviour in both classes increased by around 15%.

The teachers were then shown another video sequence (again from BATSAC) in which effective (private and specific) praising was demonstrated. They were asked to copy this procedure, aiming to give at least 15 praise statements per lesson and to go on with their practice of reprimanding privately. As a result, the amount of time spent on-task increased by a further 10% to more than 80%. This is a satisfactory level, being the average for secondary classes according to our research, reported in Chapter Two.

The other two teachers participating in the study taught older pupils, fourth and fifth year classes. During initial observations it was found that neither of them gave very much feedback at all to their pupils by way of reprimand or praise. The procedures followed were the same as those applied with the first two teachers except that they were asked first to practise private praise and then to use private reprimands. Initially, they were asked to give twenty private and specific praise statements per lesson. On-task behaviour rose by about 12% in both classes as a result, to just over

80%, and increased by a further 7% when the teachers were asked to employ up to five private reprimands per lesson as well.

Follow-up checks which were carried out some eight weeks later revealed a most pleasing picture. The fifth year class had left by this time but in the other three classes teachers had maintained their high rates of positive reinforcement and their new ways of reprimanding. Levels of pupil on-task behaviour remained high in all three classes. Taken together, the results for the four teachers confirm that there is a role for reprimands if used sparingly, specifically and privately and in a context which is generally positive.

These simple experimental interventions demonstrate first that teachers can change their behaviour by altering the way in which they respond to their pupils. Under guidance they can learn to become more effective givers of encouragement and, within this context, to exercise more effective control of misbehaviour. Secondly, the experiments showed that when teachers changed their behaviour, pupils' behaviour changed too. This resulted in classroom conditions which were more agreeable to both teachers and students and which were likely to be more conducive to good academic outcomes.

We can keep our use of reprimands to a low level by employing alternative, more positive strategies. Positive teachers seek to avoid conflict wherever possible. Instead of using reprimands teachers can simply ignore some trivial incidents completely. The use of reprimands may often prove to be counter-productive since we know that the inappropriate behaviour of some pupils is reinforced by the attention they get from teacher reprimands (so-called attention seeking behaviour). If teachers continually comment adversely on every minor misdemeanour they can sometimes make matters worse.

One of our students carried out an intriguing small-scale study which again demonstrates the importance of teacher praise and approval. An experienced female social studies teacher was observed teaching a mixed ability class of 17 fourth year pupils in a West Midlands comprehensive school. The first three observations showed that she was a very positive teacher, giving nearly twice as many positive as negative responses to her pupils. It is not surprising that her class averaged around 95% of their time on-task, working and behaving appropriately. The teacher was then asked if she would try to change her teaching behaviour by giving little or no praise but to increase her use of reprimands to comment on instances of misbehaviour.

Perhaps surprisingly, she agreed to this request and was observed for a further three sessions. During this period she gave only four positive responses but doubled her use of reprimands. The effect on her class was dramatic. Class on-task behaviour dropped to an average of only 78% and was clearly falling. She found this deterioration very stressful and so it was agreed that she should resume her normal teaching style. She was then observed for a further session and once again she used twice as many positive as negative comments. Her pupils' on-task behaviour immediately returned to a high level, around 89%.

This is a telling study made possible only by the confidence of a good, positive teacher. Although only small scale it confirms some early American research which demonstrated how good classes could be made more disruptive by reducing praise and increasing reprimands. The message is clear. Keep your praise rates high and minimise the use of reprimands (ignoring altogether some trivial misbehaviours) if you want to enjoy good classroom discipline. Before leaving this topic, however, we would not want to give the impression that ignoring, used on its own, is some sort of panacea. We are concerned that some educational psychologists have, in the past, over-emphasised the importance of ignoring and have not stressed sufficiently that it will only be effective when used in conjunction with other, more positive procedures. We will return to this point again in Chapter Five when we discuss the powerful behaviour management strategy known as rules, praise and ignoring.

Another alternative to reprimanding a pupil for misbehaving is to ask him or her, in a neutral tone of voice, what he or she should be doing. This serves two purposes. First, the articulation of the nature of the task by the pupil may prompt the appropriate behaviour. Secondly, this may reveal a genuine misunderstanding that the pupil is experiencing about the nature of the work. Clearly, if they do not know exactly what they have to do pupils are more likely to misbehave. Many good teachers have other, more positive ways of dealing with misbehaviour than using reprimands. Some use humour to good effect to defuse the situation. It must be emphasised, however, that we do mean humour, not sarcasm.

Finally, we should remember, especially when dealing with older pupils in the secondary school, that these young people will shortly be adults and deserve to be treated accordingly. The abrupt manner of speaking, sometimes verging on rudeness, that some teachers employ can be quite offensive to other adults let alone sensitive adolescents. We would recommend that teachers should think carefully about how they would deal with a problem situation if the miscreants involved were, indeed, other adults. For example, we would not embarrass colleagues by criticising their dress sense or by reminding them, in front of friends, that they had neglected to return a book when it was urgently needed. Some things we just would not say at all and with other issues we would pick our time very carefully.

A point which we have already made and which summarises all of our suggested strategies for dealing with misbehaviour is "Act, don't react". By this we mean that teachers should think carefully and in advance about how they are going to respond to trouble-some behaviour. Rather than reacting emotionally without think-ing, teachers should try to respond in a considered manner worthy of a professional.

Improving your positives

As we have already intimated, it follows logically that if you can increase the amount of time that pupils spend behaving appropri-ately there is less time for them to behave inappropriately. By accentuating the positive we can reduce the necessity for nega-tives. In this section we will consider how we can improve our use of praise so as to make it more effective.

Praise is most effective when it is sincere and natural. Some people seem to use more praise than others but we all use praise sometimes and we can all improve our rate of praising. As we have said before, we should aim to use a variety of praise statements and make use of appropriate gestures and actions to accompany them. Similarly, we need to be sensitive in our use of praise. Our survey showed that older pupils prefer quiet, private praise but it is important to avoid appearing to be patronising.

One of the most powerful groups of reinforcers is the social response of adults, like attention and praise, physical closeness and facial expressions, like smiling. Note that here we are not referring to general pleasantness or otherwise of teachers' attitudes and contacts with children but the specific use of social reinforcers to bring about change in behaviour. What matters is when the teacher praises whom and for what behaviour.

As suggested earlier, some people are very good at making these social responses towards others and we all use them sometimes but, we can all learn to use them more effectively. Most teachers seem to believe that they are already very positive in their responses to their pupils but, as we have shown in Chapter Two, this is not true of all. We have to remember also that many of our pupils have not yet learned to recognise and respond to the rather subtle social signals that adults use to communicate their feelings about each other. This is not a cause for despair but rather a challenge to our skills in teaching. We may have to teach adolescents how to engage the attention of adults, how to address them, how to express an alternative point of view without giving offence, how to break off an exchange politely and so on. This too can, and should, be done positively, not by nagging and chiding.

When using praise and rewards we need to consider what can be said, how it can be said and what we can use as a source of positive reinforcement. How we say these things or carry out these actions is almost as important as what we say or do. If you are not sure how enthusiastic you look when doing or saying these things try using a mirror; in private, of course! There is no doubt that practice will improve one's ability to dispense positive social reinforcement effectively and it costs nothing.

Generally speaking it has been found that statements of both praise and blame are most effective in bringing about change in pupils' behaviour when they take the form of what we call REX responses. Such responses can be regarded as belonging to one of three categories although the distinction between them is not of great importance. If the classroom is one where rules have been agreed and are clearly manifest it is possible for the teacher to refer to the fact that a pupil has succeeded in carrying out an agreed rule. The teacher can say, "Thanks Susan, you've remembered our rule about putting up your hand." This would be an example of an R response where the teacher had related praise to the keeping of an agreed rule. Sometimes teachers couple praise with drawing attention to a pupil's work or behaviour in terms of setting a good example. Such E responses are quite common in practical subjects when the teacher wants to draw attention to the fact that a certain student has performed well or produced a good example of the work set. Some secondary teachers use display areas in order to exhibit work they feel is of special worth and this should be encouraged. At other times they may send the pupil to a senior member of staff to show what has been achieved or an improvement that has been made.

The third category of REX responses (X responses) comprises cases where teachers spell out precisely (eXactly) what it is that they are pleased about. In a sense the two preceding cases do just this, but in a particular way. By using an X response the teacher makes it clear to the pupil what they are pleased about. Some teachers give quite a high level of positive responses in terms of saying "Good" or "Well done", but the pupils are sometimes not quite sure what they have been praised for. Is it the appearance of the work, the quantity that has been produced or the fact that most of it has been completed correctly? It is very important that pupils should know exactly what they are being praised or blamed for.

It is worth repeating our earlier point that verbal comment, whether of praise or blame, should be directed at the act performed, rather than at the person who has performed it. There is a great deal of difference between commenting on a good or bad act and saying that you are a bad or good person. To imply that a pupil is a bad person lays us open to the charge of labelling. We know well enough that once a pupil acquires a reputation for being bad it tends to become a self-fulfilling prophecy. Teachers begin to expect such pupils to behave badly and to look for corroborating evidence for their expectations whilst the individuals themselves begin to regard themselves as marked out for special attention. Both eventualities are to be avoided. Likewise, it does a pupil no good to be regarded as special because of a reputation for good work or behaviour. It can place unwarranted strain on a pupil from both staff and fellow students.

It is important for teachers to be aware of how much positive reinforcement they are using and how many negative consequences they are providing. One way of doing this is to use a hand tally-counter to record positive and negative responses as described in Chapter Two. Of course, if you are counting negatives the fact that you are holding the tally counter in your hand is bound to inhibit your giving of negative responses to your pupils. Just as you are about to shout at someone for inappropriate behaviour you will be aware of the tally counter and will refrain. The result will not be a very accurate count of your usual number of negative responses but that does not matter if your intention is to reduce them. On the other hand, if you are counting your positive responses with a view to increasing their number, the tally counter will again be a cue for you to be positive because every time you are positive you will be able to notch up one more tally. It will encourage you to look for appropriate behaviour and to reinforce it.

We routinely ask our students to carry out exercises in which they record their use of positives and negatives. For example, one of our student teachers decided to monitor her own performance on teaching practice using a tally counter. During the first week she made no effort to change her behaviour and recorded, on average, six positives and 16 negatives during her 15-minute self-observation periods. She then attempted to change her own behaviour over the following four weeks and with great success. She managed to increase her positives to just over 13 and her use of negatives dropped to around four, per session, on average. To put it another way, she changed from using nearly three times as many negatives as positives to using more than three times as many positives as negatives. If a young student teacher can achieve results like these when under the stress of teaching practice, it should be possible for experienced teachers to do at least as well. We appreciate, of course, that experienced teachers may well have some unlearning to do.

Using a tally-counter certainly makes you more aware of the nature of your responses but if you really want to know how many positive and negative responses you give in a typical lesson, and this is interesting information for any teacher, then you really need to have somebody else to do the observing for you. Perhaps you can find a colleague who will watch you for a period and give you some objective feedback (using a tally counter, maybe) and then you can change places on another occasion. In addition, it would be salutary for all of us to have someone count how many opportunities we miss of applying a positive response appropriately to good work or behaviour and how often we give a reward when little has been done to deserve it. The same can apply in the opposite direction to the negative consequences we employ. Another way of getting some more objective feedback rather than using the tally counter yourself is to make a tape-recording of your lesson and then listen to it later on. Of course, this will only pick up the verbal responses you make but these will probably include most of the responses you make to your pupils.

What appears to be critical about the response rates of teachers is the ratio between positive and negative responses. Clearly there will be certain optimum rates of responding. On the one hand some teachers are very non-responsive whilst some submit their pupils to a barrage of comment and feedback. The appropriate level of comment from teachers will vary from situation to situation and from teacher to teacher but it would appear that where good teaching and learning is taking place positive comment usually far outweighs the negative. In cases where the balance has been predominantly negative and where teachers have managed to change this, a change in the level of pupil on-task behaviour has been observed to follow. For example, one of our students, an experienced teacher, carried out a useful study with a student teacher on final teaching practice. Preliminary observations revealed that the student teacher was using almost three times as many negative as positive responses. She was then instructed in the basic principles of Positive Teaching and decided that she would attempt to provide more positive responses to her pupils and to reduce her use of negatives. Subsequent observations showed that she was able to change her behaviour markedly, now giving eight times as many positive as negative responses. As a result pupil on-task behaviour increased from around 55% to nearly 75%. When she was observed again a few weeks later on-task behaviour was still over 70%.

Similarly, another of our students observed a male mathematics teacher with his first year class of 28 below-average pupils. Preliminary observations over five lessons revealed that the teacher used twice as many negatives as positives and that pupils spent only about 50% of their time on-task, actually getting on with their work. He then agreed "to try to catch the children being good" and to praise them in an overt way for appropriate behaviour. At the same time he was to try to reduce his use of negatives. Observations of the next five sessions revealed that he was now using nearly four times as many positives as negatives and the on-task behaviour of the class had risen to over 78%, on average. This improvement was brought about very easily and we may note that overt praise for good behaviour was effective with these younger pupils.

Yet another of our students persuaded a chemistry teacher to change her teaching behaviour in a similar way with two fifth year classes (with 12 and 15 pupils in each class respectively) both of which she taught twice a week. Observations of the first class for two weeks showed that the pupils were on-task for about 71% of the time. She was then asked to increase her use of positive comments to at least ten every 15 minutes and the class was observed for a further two weeks. During this period she was encouraged to use such positive comments as, "You have worked well today" or "I'm impressed with the way you work together " or "That was a very useful observation". Pupil on-task behaviour rose to 88%. She was then asked to return to her previous teaching style for two more weeks and on-task behaviour was observed to fall back to around 76%. Meanwhile, over the same period, she was also observed teaching the second class. At first, she was observed teaching this class in her usual way, even after she had changed her behaviour with the other class. The behaviour of this class remained fairly constant throughout the four week period at around 77%. When she changed her teaching behaviour to include more positives with this class, and was observed for two more weeks, on-task behaviour was seen to rise to around 93%. This small-scale study shows that simple praise strategies work well even with older pupils. Note also that the improvements in behaviour with each class occurred only when the teacher increased her use of praise and, in the first class, behaviour deteriorated again when she stopped.

Supplementing praise with other strategies

The effective use of praise and encouragement will probably be sufficient to bring about a co-operative atmosphere conducive to learning for many classes for most of the time. Occasionally, however, we encounter pupils or even whole classes which do not respond so readily. Alternatively, even with well-motivated pupils and classes, there will be times when the teacher may wish to encourage even greater effort or to teach other, more mature social behaviours. In these cases we may wish to supplement praise with other strategies including, perhaps, the use of other rewards.

Some visual record of progress is a good provider of reinforcement. This is the function of wall-charts showing tokens of achievement but inter-pupil rivalry is not generally part of Positive Teaching. Teachers already use tokens of some sort (points or stars, perhaps) in order to motivate their pupils and allow competition between groups in order to stimulate improvement. For example, an arrangement may be made by which the winning of points or tokens depends upon improvement in work or behaviour. However, teachers frequently arrange matters so that the reward goes to the group which gets most points. This is fine so long as the competition is close, but once the members of one group observe that they are far behind the rest with no chance of catching up, all the motivational effect for them disappears. If there is to be an element of winning, it must be open to all, equally. Rather than promising a reward of some sort to the team or individual getting the best score it is better to set a reasonable target such that all who reach that criterion may have access to the rewarding consequences. By this means everyone is in the race until the end and, as in the caucus race in *Alice in Wonderland*, it is possible for everyone to be a winner so long as they make an effort to improve.

From our survey, reported earlier, we should remember that free time is highly valued by secondary pupils of all ages and that a positive letter home is the next most highly valued. Younger pupils also value house points as a reward. These and other rewards such as the opportunity to choose an activity, listen to music or to use special apparatus can all be used to supplement praise. But a little imagination and discussion with pupils will generate a host of other rewarding activities and special treats which can be given on an occasional basis to a class which continues to work well. We have heard of positive teachers who organise baked bean toasted sandwich parties and horror video sessions at half-term for classes which work well. This may not be your style but you can probably come up with equally appealing alternatives.

The best competition for a pupil is with him or herself in comparison with earlier performance. Most adolescents are at a stage when they are beginning to be self-critical. Some are too prone to this practice and become over-anxious as a result but most are well able to record their own progress in academic output or in social behaviour if they are shown how and they are usually very willing and interested to do it. A truly objective record of their own performance would give them a much more realistic base from which to judge their own progress. We will return to this important issue of self-recording in Chapter Five where we will also discuss other effective classroom strategies for teaching and maintaining high levels of appropriate classroom behaviour.

Further reading

Further details of our work on pupil preferences for varying forms of reward and punishment are reported in the following two articles:

Houghton, S., Merrett, F. and Wheldall, K. (1988). The attitudes of British secondary school pupils to praise, rewards, punishment and reprimands. *New Zealand Journal of Educational Studies, 23,* 203-214.

Sharpe, P., Wheldall, K. and Merrett, F. (1987). The attitudes of British secondary school pupils to praise and reward. *Educational Studies, 13,* 293-302.

Our work on private praise and reprimands is described in:

Houghton, S., Wheldall, K., Jukes, R. and Sharpe, A. (1989). The effects of limited private reprimands and increased private praise on classroom behaviour in four British secondary school classes. Birmingham University: Centre for Child Study.

Chapter Five
DEVELOPING EFFECTIVE
CLASSROOM STRATEGIES

Good classroom behaviour will not necessarily ensure effective academic learning but it is, in our view, an essential prerequisite. Clearly, pupils will find it more difficult to work in a noisy and disruptive environment. Positive Teaching, as we have tried to make clear throughout this book, is concerned with identifying and increasing appropriate behaviour in the classroom. Positive Teaching is not about being repressive in order to reduce unacceptable behaviour. We reject the notion of the teacher as a form of Dalek continually on the look-out for misbehaviour in order to exterminate it. In this chapter we will be discussing how teachers can develop effective classroom strategies for encouraging appropriate behaviour.

Before we progress to this, however, let us consider certain key issues which underpin the whole enterprise. If we are attempting to teach certain new forms of behaviour or to increase the rate of behaviours which already occur but only infrequently, then there are several important ground rules which must be applied. Whatever is chosen as a reinforcer must be applied:

1. Contingently. It must be arranged so that the reinforcer follows the behaviour every time it occurs but is not available otherwise. For example, a modern languages teacher makes sure that a point is given every time a first year pupil responds in French with a complete sentence, but not otherwise.

2. Immediately. There must be no waiting between the act and the reinforcer as there would be in the situation where the teacher tries to motivate the student by saying, "If you study hard for the whole term you will be able to pass the examination". Consider here what is meant by study hard in terms of pin-pointing behaviour. So many of the rewards which are

offered by education and in schools generally are of this long-term nature and do not constitute proper rewards at all in the context of Positive Teaching. Think of some of the pupils you teach and consider how the school is rewarding them day by day for efforts that they may be making to improve their work or behaviour. Your most probable conclusion will be "not a lot". Praise and rewards can both be given immediately.

3. Consistently. This is one of the chief elements in Positive Teaching. If children find that they are allowed to behave in a certain way on one day whilst on the next they are punished for the same behaviour, they are being deprived of the opportunity of finding out how the rule system works. A pupil can learn the rules which operate in a particular situation only if the consequences can be relied upon. Many pupils who have difficulty in behaving appropriately in the classroom have come from previous regimes (the home, for example) which lacked such consistency, so that to provide a consistent regime for all pupils should be one of the chief aims of positive teachers. This is, of course, more difficult in secondary schools where pupils experience continual changes of teacher expectation and of teaching style as they move from lesson to lesson. These problems may be reduced where the teachers have opted for Positive Teaching, perhaps following attendance at a training course such as BATSAC, described later in this chapter.

4. Abundantly. The first few steps made by the pupil which are recognised to be in the right direction must be given abundant reward. This is probably not going to be easy because pupils who do not perform very well or whose behaviour is rather poor are not going to make sudden and large-scale improvements at first. The improvements that such pupils are likely to make will be very small; hardly discernible, perhaps, unless the teacher is a very good and practised observer. This is why Positive Teaching places such stress on the importance of careful pin-pointing, counting and recording of behaviour. To begin with, every instance of appropriate behaviour should be

rewarded at once because this has been found to be the most effective way to bring about change in behaviour.

Once the desired behaviour has been learned and is occurring frequently enough the task of the positive teacher has changed. He or she now has the job of maintaining the newly learned behaviour and for that different procedures are needed. It has been found that the best way of maintaining behaviour once it has been learned is to provide intermittent reinforcement as a consequence rather than the continuous and abundant reinforcement necessary to teach it in the first place. This is done by arranging for reinforcement to occur less frequently and less immediately. In other words, we allow a leaner rate of reinforcement to be adopted so that in time two or three good responses may be required to obtain a reward and, by degrees, the pupil is made to wait longer for the reward to come. This process of gradually reducing the relative level of rewarding by small amounts (known as fading) should then continue until the behaviours are maintained by the infrequent rewards which occur naturally and which serve to maintain most human social conduct.

It must be stressed that it is very important that these changes in the rewarding process should be made very gradually. They should not be started until the new behaviour has been thoroughly learned and care must be taken to see that there is no falling off while the fading process is under way. If fading begins too soon or happens too quickly then ground won will soon be lost. We can see how behaviour is maintained by natural consequences by use of a simple example. It is only occasionally that people respond to our courteous waiting for them to pass through a doorway first but it does happen sometimes and that is enough to maintain our behaviour. It is worth mentioning at this stage that teachers are not into the business of making saints. We do not expect perfect behaviour from our pupils but rather a standard that is reasonable both for them and for others. Of paramount importance in all our dealings with young people are the principles of justice and consistency. Nothing upsets them more than to realise that they are being treated unfairly. Rules of conduct apply to all, to us as well as the young people we teach.

A common reaction to Positive Teaching, however, is that such an approach would only work with young children. Many teachers are sceptical of success in secondary settings, believing that at best it would necessitate highly complex and time-consuming procedures. We have now carried out a number of studies which demonstrate the effectiveness of simple strategies with classes of older, secondary school children.

The methods we advocate are all firmly based on the principles of Positive Teaching and have all been carefully and rigorously tried and tested in work with teachers. Simple and straightforward interventions by teachers using positive methods can bring about dramatic results in terms of improved classroom atmosphere and the quantity and quality of work produced. Both antecedents and consequences can be used to good effect to change behaviour. Moreover, these methods , illustrated in the case studies below, have been shown to yield more satisfying and rewarding classroom experiences for both teachers and children.

Positive Teaching can be applied in the management of classroom social behaviour in an endless variety of ways, calling for imagination, inventiveness and initiative on the part of teachers. There is no single prescriptive nostrum. Positive Teaching requires the consistent application of basic principles to unique and personal classroom problems.

In this first example, a religious studies teacher was keen to increase the rate of oral responding with a second year class and used a previously hidden talent as an effective reinforcer. Observations of the class over six lessons had shown that fewer than 50% of pupils were volunteering to answer questions. The teacher then offered to perform a conjuring trick every time everyone in the class had answered a question. The pupils found this very appealing and now began to work to ensure that everybody attempted to answer a question. This resulted in over 80% of the pupils, on average, now contributing to the lesson.

Another useful device is to couple classroom rules with the giving of feedback to pupils, as in the following example. This study was carried out with a mixed-ability fourth year group who were following a GCSE course in history. The pupils found this course very demanding and rarely responded in question and answer sessions. Observations of the (male) teacher and his class over four lessons showed that few pupils ever volunteered to answer questions and that most of the questions were answered by just one boy. The class received this news with shock. The teacher explained the importance of questioning (and answering) in lessons and negotiated four rules with the pupils for future sessions. These were as follows:

1.   We listen to the teacher's question.

2.   We raise our hands to answer without talking.

3.   We keep our hands up until someone is chosen to answer.

4.   We listen to the answer.

For the next six lessons the pupils were reminded of the rules at the beginning of each lesson and a feedback table was posted following each lesson showing how well each pupil had done in terms of hand raising and in responding if called upon. This simple procedure (which did, however, require an observer) resulted in over 25% responding to any one question and well over 50% of the class responding at some point in the lesson.

Implementing rules, praise and ignoring

The last study leads on logically to one of the most useful and widely used techniques in Positive Teaching known as RPI or rules, praise and ignoring. In brief, it requires the teacher first to negotiate with pupils a set of three or four short, positively phrased rules covering acceptable classroom behaviour, as described in Chapter Three. These often take the form of simple declarations of intent such as, "We try to get on with our work quietly" or "We put up our hands when we want to ask a question". Thinking in terms of the ABC model we outlined earlier it will be appreciated that rules are being employed here as important antecedents for behaviour. They act as a form of prompt or cue for appropriate behaviour. Teachers operating RPI are encouraged to draw attention to the rules regularly, preferably when pupils are clearly keeping the rules, but not when they are being infringed.

Both praise and ignoring refer to the consequences aspect of this procedure. Quite simply, teachers are required to praise pupils for keeping the rules (catch them being good) and to ignore infractions. Praise may refer to the whole class or to individuals but should refer specifically to their behaviour in keeping the rules.

As we have said, ignoring is often more difficult for teachers and is frequently misunderstood. It refers only to the behaviours governed by the rules and does not mean that teachers should not intervene if a fight breaks out or if pupils are about to do something dangerous. The idea is to avoid responding to rule-related misbehaviours since to do so may be counter-productive if the pupils involved find any form of teacher attention rewarding. It also detracts from the overall positive approach.

It must be emphasised that ignoring on its own (without rules and praise) is unlikely to be effective and as a technique it has certainly been over-sold to teachers. "Ignore it and it will go away" is the sloppy advice sometimes given to teachers by advisers and educational psychologists. This is, of course, total nonsense to professionals who know that they cannot permit certain behaviour excesses to continue without intervention and who recognise that their attention to certain behaviours, such as those involved in showing off to peers, has little effect in comparison with peer approval or attention. An unsuccessful or unpopular child who gets a little begrudging acceptance or a laugh from his or her peers for fooling about is often not going to be much affected by teacher reprimand or by ignoring. The technique of ignoring is at least partly predicated upon the assumption that teacher attention (even if negative) may be rewarding. The hard truth is that teacher response may be irrelevant.

In Chapter Three, we described one of our studies in which a headteacher improved the on-task behaviour of the class of 14-15 year-old pupils he took for remedial maths simply by providing more maths problems for those who finished quickly. It was decided that on-task behaviour could be improved still more and two additional, alternative strategies were agreed upon and implemented. On the first, and thereafter on every other day, a simple RPI strategy was employed. The rules for this were as follows:

1. When the teacher is talking to us we look at him.

2. We get on with our work quietly.

3. We try not to stop others from working.

4. We try to pay attention to our work and try not to daydream.

These were printed on card, read out at the beginning of every lesson and also, on occasion, referred to during the lesson but not when infractions of the rules occurred. Infringements of the rules were ignored unless these were serious or dangerous. On the other hand the teacher was instructed to look out for pupils keeping the rules, individually or collectively, and to lose no opportunity for praising them by saying, for example, "It's good to see Errol, David and Patrick getting on with their work", "Susan is concentrating well", "This is good, I can see you are all getting on really well".

In addition to this basic RPI programme a timer game was introduced, on alternate days, where points were awarded for on-task behaviour. Basically, this meant that a cassette was played which emitted a chime on average every two minutes. The chimes were a signal to the teacher to look up to see if the pupils were observing the rules. If they were, he awarded a point and praised the class. Each point was worth one minute of free time during the last maths lesson of the week on Friday afternoon. Scoring 25 points would win the whole lesson off. During the free period the children could chat quietly but freely or play games such as draughts or cards which were supplied.

As we reported in Chapter Three, average on-task behaviour rose by nearly 15% to an average of 69%, after more maths problems were put up on the board. The two new procedures improved behaviour even more. On the odd days when the RPI strategy alone was employed, average on-task behaviour increased to over 80% and by yet another 10% on even days when the timer game was played. It should be noted, however, that after twelve lessons the levels for the two new procedures merged at around 95% average on-task behaviour.

This study gives a firm indication that relatively simple, non-intrusive positive strategies such as setting extra work and RPI can be very effective at the secondary level although the teacher found that ignoring some behaviours was quite difficult. Doubt is thus cast on the common sense view that praise may be counter-productive with adolescents. Another aspect of this study which may call for comment is the use of free time as a reinforcer. It was the opinion of the headteacher who took part in this study that more work was done in the four lessons for which the intervention was in operation than in the five lessons occupied by maths previously.

We subsequently carried out a second study in which RPI was again used, this time with pupils in four third-year home economics classes all in the same secondary school. Four rules were adopted as follows:

1. We try to work quietly and put up our hands when we need help.

2. We listen carefully to instructions and read the board and our recipe sheets carefully.

3. We try to work tidily in our units and share the jobs when clearing away.

4. We get on with our cooking without disturbing others.

Since the RPI procedures were to be employed in cookery lessons, reprimands for potentially dangerous behaviour were not excluded. Teachers were, however, instructed to ignore rule infringements wherever possible and to concentrate on praising rule-keeping and on-task behaviours. To back up RPI in this study, the teachers were also asked to make a general evaluative summary statement at the end of each lesson concerning the behaviour of the class during that lesson; for example, "You have all worked much harder today than last week. Let's see if you can do even better next time".

All four classes had gained a reputation for noisiness, untidiness and not listening. The aims of the study were to encourage more attention to the task in hand and, especially, to reduce the excessive noise levels commonly experienced in such practical classes. To this end the four classes were systematically observed over an eight week period and levels of on-task behaviour were recorded. In addition, it was possible to obtain objective measures of noise level by using a decibel meter.

RPI was introduced successively at two-week intervals with three of the four classes. All classes were observed operating normally for the first two weekly lessons and the intervention was then introduced in the first class. Two weeks later it was introduced into the second class and after a further two weeks into the third class. The fourth class remained under normal conditions throughout.

In each of the three classes in which RPI was employed, average levels of on-task behaviour rose following the introduction of the intervention; in the first class from (on average) around 78% to 83%, more markedly in the second class from around 75% to 89% and in the third class from about 75% to 85%. In the fourth class, where no intervention was attempted, on-task behaviour remained fairly constant at about 83% throughout. The effects of the strategy were shown even more clearly on noise level. Again, in each of the first three classes noise level was shown to fall markedly following the introduction of the intervention; in the first class from an average of around 66 dB to 62 dB, in the second class from 68 dB to 63 dB and in third class from 69 dB to 61 dB. In the fourth class noise level remained roughly constant at around 63 dB. This study provides convincing evidence of the effectiveness of behavioural methods with secondary aged children in a potentially difficult practical work setting, most previous studies in secondary schools having been carried out in academic lessons.

Yet another RPI study was carried out by one of our students with a rather noisy, disruptive, second-year class of 26 pupils. Two teachers took part in the study; one taught them English and the other religious education.

Preliminary observations were made of both teachers with the class for six weeks, each teacher being observed once per week. RPI was then introduced to the class when taught by the English teacher. The rules which were negotiated with the pupils and then written into their exercise books were as follows:

1. Listen quietly and carefully when the teacher is talking.

2. Put your hand up when you want to ask a question or contribute to the class discussion.

3. Settle to work quickly and quietly.

4. Be pleasant and polite to each other.

Observations were made of both teachers weekly for a further six weeks. RPI was then withdrawn and again both teachers were observed. In the religious education lessons the teacher gave nearly twice as many positives as negatives and the average level of on-task behaviour of the class was around 75%. No attempt was made to change this teacher's behaviour towards his pupils during any part of the study. His natural style with pupils was to be firm in instruction and to encourage the pupils by praising their good work and behaviour whilst largely ignoring poor work and disruptive events. In a sense, he was already carrying out a kind of rules, praise and ignoring regime. There was no apparent change in pupil on-task behaviour over the 14 lessons in which he was observed.

On the other hand, the English teacher was asked to change her behaviour since during preliminary observations she was clearly giving rather more negatives than positives and the on-task level of her class averaged only 56%. During RPI she gave about the same number of positive comments as before but far fewer negatives so that she now gave twice as many positives as negatives. This was very similar to the teacher of religious education and as a result the average on-task level for the class rose to nearly 77%, again similar to that in the religious education lessons. As soon as the RPI intervention was abandoned, however, the English teacher's behaviour changed again. Negatives were again exceeding positives whilst the average on-task level for the class fell to about 64%. These results demonstrate very clearly the power of the RPI intervention and of its influence over the behaviour of both teacher and class.

We have carried out numerous other studies using RPI with our students. A most interesting study was carried out in a large inner-city comprehensive school in the West Midlands. The study was undertaken with a mixed-ability class of 27 first year pupils who were especially troublesome to most of the eleven teachers who taught them throughout the week. Many of these teachers were senior members of staff and there was a general consensus that TOOT and HOC were the most frequent troublesome behaviours.

Six teachers were observed teaching this class on at least three occasions and average on-task levels varied between 71% and 84% except in maths where the average on-task level was only 68%. The maths teacher undertook to try to carry out an intervention in order to improve the pupils' work rate. First, for four weeks, rules were negotiated and rules, praise and ignoring was tried. The teacher managed to reduce her average number of negatives from about 12 to 4.5 and increase her positives from 2 to 12. Accordingly, the pupils' on-task level rose to 75%. During the next four weeks the RPI was formalised into a timer game strategy. When a signal (occurring at irregular intervals) was heard the teacher looked at one of the three groups into which the class had been divided (the order being randomised) and if all members of that group were keeping the rules the teacher praised them and awarded them a point. Groups were set a target score which, if attained, resulted in each pupil getting a merit token. Merit tokens were part of an effective incentive scheme already in operation in the school.

The importance of the ratio between the levels of approving and disapproving has already been referred to. It is interesting to note that in this study the teachers with whom relatively high on-task levels were associated when teaching this class had positive to negative ratios which were even, i.e. 1:1 or with a good balance on the positive side. The teacher of mathematics had a ratio of 1:0.2 (i.e five times more negatives than positives) and an initial on-task level of 68%, the poorest of all to begin with. With RPI in operation this ratio improved to about 1:3 with a rise in on-task level to 75%. Once the timer game was working the teacher's ratio improved still further to 1:6 and the mean level of pupils' on-task behaviour rose to 87%, the highest recorded for any teacher with this class.

Another study was carried out with a male teacher and his group of 29 second year pupils of lower than average ability who were troublesome to many of his colleagues. Three simple, positive rules were agreed and for five lessons the teacher applied the rules, praise and ignore techniques. His ratio of positive to negative responses improved from 1:0.8 to 1:66! The average on-task level rose, not surprisingly perhaps, from 75% to 93%. In the next six lessons the teacher attempted gradually to reduce the number of positives he was giving. His ratio of responses became 1:9 and the on-task level dropped back to an average level of 87%. The process of fading reinforcement, that is, reducing it gradually, led to a falling off in time spent working but it was still at an acceptable level and the fading process allowed the teacher to function at a lower and, perhaps, more natural level of reinforcement.

Yet another study with a first year class of 15 low ability groups also showed how pupils responded well to RPI. In this case, the agreed rules were referred to at the beginning of every lesson. Preliminary observations over five lessons revealed an average on-task level of 59% which rose to 73% and was still rising at the end of five further sessions.

Another RPI intervention was carried out with a group of 18 third year pupils being taught German by a senior teacher. Preliminary observations showed that the teacher's ratio of response was 1:0.6 and the pupil's mean on-task behaviour level was 52%. The teacher then defined some simple positive rules and began to praise pupils for keeping these, ignoring any minor infringements. During the next four observation sessions his response ratio became 1:12 and on-task behaviour rose to 89%. During the next four lessons the teacher reverted to his earlier style of teaching. His response ratio reverted to 1:2.2 (still better than it had been) and pupils' mean on-task level fell once again, this time to 58%.

The last study to be reported concerns older pupils: 24 girls of rather below average ability taking commerce classes and it was carried out by a student teacher. The group as a whole were slow to settle to their task and spent a lot of time chatting, borrowing each other's equipment and generally hindering the progress of their peers. Observations over one week showed that the average level of on-task behaviour was a very low 48%. The first part of this study was concerned to break up friendship groups by re-allocating the girls to seats chosen randomly by the teacher. In the following three sessions on-task behaviour averaged 62%, a decided improvement but still far from satisfactory. Rules were now discussed with the group and five were agreed. The application of a praise and ignore strategy to these agreed rules resulted in an average on-task level of 83% for the subsequent six lessons.

By citing so many examples of RPI in action we have tried to demonstrate the robustness of this strategy and to show how it may be applied successfully in many different teaching contexts with pupils of all ages. In our view RPI is to be recommended to all teachers as a general procedure for improving classroom behaviour.

Involving pupils by using self-recording

Pupils themselves can be directly involved in bringing about behaviour change. Secondary aged pupils can be encouraged to monitor their own behaviour and to determine whether they are on- or off-task, for example. We carried out a study involving a 13 year-old boy in the remedial department of a large modern comprehensive school. Timothy made a great deal of fuss before settling to work and took any opportunity to stop, setting himself up as a funny man to gain attention and approval from his peer group. His behaviour became disruptive if he encountered the slightest difficulty and if the teacher was not immediately available. Teacher observations of Timothy's classroom behaviour showed that most of his time was taken up in what had been defined as off-task or disruptive behaviour. He was very shocked when he saw a graphical representation of these results. He had not realised that he "wasted so much time", as he put it and asked, "What are we going to do about it?" Because of his obvious concern and his relative maturity it was decided that he should be involved in the monitoring of the intervention, by self-recording.

Timothy was very fond of using a Doodle Art sketch pad to colour in a cartoon picture and access to this was made contingent upon improved on-task behaviour. The boy was accordingly given the opportunity to tally his own on-task behaviour with an observation schedule just like the one his teacher had used. An audible signal on a tape-recorder which occurred 30 times in half an hour, but at irregular intervals, was the cue for Timothy to record whether he was on-task or not. Ten tally marks could be exchanged for two minutes of the rewarding activity, i.e. colouring in the Doodle Art picture. It is interesting to note that after a week or so of using the observation schedule he complained about having to stop working in order to self-record! This problem was solved by giving him a tally counter to use instead. On-task behaviour rose from an average level of approximately 30% to over 60% as a result of this self-recording. For two weeks, when Timothy was asked not to record his own on-task behaviour, this level fell to 40% on average but rose once again to about 61% for the last two weeks when the programme was reintroduced. The programme was allowed to lapse at the end of the term but when the teacher measured Timothy's on-task behaviour level six weeks into the next term she found that it had improved still further and was being been maintained at a high level (around 70%).

Later, the teacher introduced the self-recording procedures to the rest of the class with very good results. The other pupils in the class had observed how Timothy's behaviour and class work had improved to his and their advantage. For example, he no longer acted as the class clown and distracted them from their own work. They were quite keen to try out the same procedure for themselves to see how it would work for them. The amount of time the pupils now spent getting on with their work increased markedly. Samples of work done by pupils before and after the intervention were compared and these showed that improvements had been made in both amount and quality of work completed.

One of our students subsequently carried out another self-recording study with a low-ability third year pupil, described as "an absolute pest" and "an interfering nuisance" by some members of staff. It was decided to observe Nick during biology and physics lessons. Once preliminary observations had been made during four lessons a rules, praise and ignoring (RPI) intervention was established for the whole class in the biology lessons. Rules were drawn up by discussion with the class but RPI was maintained on its own for only two lessons. Whilst the average on-task level for the whole class immediately rose from around 60% to over 80% following RPI, Nick's behaviour remained unchanged at about 45%. After this Nick was required to self-record his own on-task behaviour by marking a card on hearing a tape-recorded signal, as in the previous study. In the physics lessons the RPI programme was not attempted but Nick was required to carry out his self-recording as in biology.

The effect of self-recording on Nick's on-task behaviour was positive and immediate. In biology lessons his average on-task level rose from 45% to 82% whilst in physics the increase was from 54% to 79%. With this improvement in on-task behaviour it was noted that Nick produced more work and that it was better presented. His on-task behaviour level became indistinguishable from that of the rest of the class. He volunteered to answer questions more frequently and in the proper manner (formerly he was likely to shout out answers inappropriately) so that generally his behaviour was seen to improve. This very welcome improvement achieved in both science periods resulted in a positive letter being sent to his home and very warm commendation being given from a senior member of staff. This is yet another example of a boy who was aware of and troubled by his behaviour and learning problems and who was prepared to co-operate in a programme designed to bring about change.

The introduction of the RPI intervention in the biology lessons led to some notable changes in the teacher's behaviour from giving only slightly more positives than negatives previously to giving four times as many positives as negatives after. These changes were reflected in higher levels of on-task behaviour of the class as a whole in biology. In physics, where RPI was not attempted the overall ratio of positives to negatives to the class did not change. When Nick began his self-recording in physics, however, the on-task levels of the class as a whole began to rise after a while, despite the fact that the teacher's levels of approval and disapproval remained much the same. This may have been due to the fact that many of the other pupils became so interested in Nick's programme that they, too, began to use the recorded signal and to record their own on-task behaviour quite voluntarily.

These examples of self-recording show how pupils experiencing behaviour difficulties can be directly involved in Positive Teaching interventions to improve their own behaviour. Another effective Positive Teaching technique for use with individuals is behavioural contracting. This procedure requires the teacher to negotiate a good behaviour contract with the pupil which ideally specifies appropriate pupil behaviours, a target for the pupil to achieve, a time period and a reward. For example, one of our students negotiated a contract with a third year pupil, Michael, to whom she taught English. Michael engaged in a lot of what we termed TOOT, HOC and OOS in Chapter One, i.e talking out of turn, hindering other children and out of seat behaviours. These behaviours were a problem only during normal English lessons, not in the drama lessons taken by the same teacher. When she showed Michael her observations of his behaviour he was concerned and, as a consequence, she negotiated with him the following contract:

> I, Michael Evans, agree to decrease my out of seat (OOS), talking out of turn (TOOT) and hindering other children (HOC) behaviour during English lessons. If I achieve a total of ten or fewer incidences during the week by half-term I will be allowed, in return, to leave ten minutes early on the last Friday afternoon. In addition, Miss Hunt will agree to give my class (3B) an extra drama lesson during the week after half-term.
>
> Signed .... Michael Evans
>
> I, Miss Hunt, agree to the above conditions.
>
> Signed .... Miss Hunt   17th January

Prior to negotiating this contract Michael averaged about 30 instances of inappropriate behaviour per English lesson but during the intervention this number fell steadily over the weeks to below five per lesson and he obtained his contracted reward. His behaviour began to deteriorate again after half-term, once the contract had been completed, climbing back to over ten instances per lesson. His teacher then told him that she was going to record his behaviour again and started praising instances of appropriate behaviour. Almost at once, his behaviour improved and instances of inappropriate behaviour dropped steadily, to below five per lesson.

Ideally, in the study above the teacher would have done better to negotiate a contract to increase appropriate, rather than to decrease inappropriate, behaviour but the technique was still clearly effective. Contracting is a useful strategy for use with individual pupils, not least because they find the notion of a contract intriguing.

The various studies reported in this chapter provide convincing evidence of the effectiveness of Positive Teaching methods with secondary aged pupils. What we are advocating here is that teachers can be both firm and positive. Neither harsh, authoritarian repression nor cloying, patronising sentimentality are congruent with the goals of real education. Our research has shown that teachers can learn to be more effective managers of pupil behaviour by following the principles and procedures of Positive Teaching. In the final section of this chapter we will describe the training package we have developed for secondary teachers through which such skills can be learned.

Training teachers to be more positive

There can no longer be any real doubt about the effectiveness of Positive Teaching approaches to problems of classroom order and discipline in secondary schools. Secondary teachers can become much more effective managers of classroom behaviour when instructed in the use of Positive Teaching techniques. During the course of our research it rapidly became clear to us that an in-service course by which groups of teachers could be trained effectively was very much needed. To this end, we set up the Positive Teaching Project at the Centre for Child Study in 1981, funded initially by the Schools Council.

We would like to conclude this introduction to Positive Teaching with a description of the training package we have developed for secondary teachers. It is based on two important assumptions. First, in order to change their pupils' classroom behaviour teachers must change their own ways of responding to pupils by learning new skills of classroom management. The second assumption follows closely from this: it is only by observing and recording changes in teacher and pupil behaviour that we can claim success for the effectiveness of our training courses. Consequently, the development of our training package has been directly governed by the results of successive evaluations based upon classroom observations. In large part the content of our package draws upon the programmes of experimental and observational classroom research we have already described.

The first course we developed was an in-service training package for primary and middle school teachers entitled the *Behavioural Approach to Teaching Package* or BATPACK, which we will not dwell on here. We subsequently went on to develop a parallel package for secondary school teachers entitled BATSAC: the *Behavioural Approach to Teaching Secondary Aged Children.* BATSAC is a skills-based course to be run on site for interested staff in a secondary school. It is made clear to teachers that BATSAC aims to teach only basic positive skills for managing classroom behaviours (it does not attempt to turn teachers into therapists) and teachers are required to contract that they will attend all sessions and complete all assignments.

The course is designed to be taught by a tutor who has attended one of our tutor training courses. Tutors must have a good working knowledge of Positive Teaching and its applications in schools. Many are educational psychologists but we are also beginning to train more teachers who have followed advanced courses in Positive Teaching. At the training course, which lasts about six hours, tutors receive a copy of a manual which contains all the detailed instructions necessary for a trained tutor to run a course.

The BATSAC course consists of six one-hour sessions called units taught at weekly intervals. A session length of one hour was judged to be as much as most teachers could tolerate at the end of a hard teaching day. The six sessions also fit neatly into a half-term. We decided to operate within these practical constraints and limited our course accordingly. Each unit has its own set of notes which teachers complete during the session. BATSAC units have been planned so that teachers do not just sit and listen to an expert giving advice. In every session course members will find themselves involved in observing, judging and commenting on important behaviour management issues. Many of these are based on video-taped sequences of classroom interactions. During the weekdays, between sessions, they will be observing carefully what is going on in their own classrooms and trying out the various strategies suggested in the previous units. In the weekly BATSAC sessions time is always given for exchange of experiences in applying the suggested strategies and for more general discussion. Encouragement is also given for questions, criticisms and comment so that there are many opportunities for teachers to learn from each other. BATSAC is, after all, the outcome of lengthy development in which feedback from teachers has played an important part. Above all, we would like to stress that standing back from your daily work and considering some of your problems afresh in collaboration with your colleagues is not only fruitful but fun.

Each unit has accompanying course reading and a research note in which an attempt is made to supply some of the theoretical material which will inform the practical skills learned in the unit and which provide the reading assignment for the week. In the last unit an attempt is made to review all the skills and techniques which have been covered and to present some successful classroom strategies tried out by other teachers in secondary schools.

BATSAC concentrates upon improving the teacher's ability to manage the classroom situation as a whole rather than the behavioural/learning problems of particular children. It attempts to do this by helping teachers to define clearly the commonest classroom behaviour problems and to observe them carefully, whilst concentrating upon positive measures to bring about change. BATSAC attempts to change teachers' responses to their classes principally by skilful attention to the teaching context and by being more positive towards specifically defined pupil behaviours which they wish to encourage. In addition to specific skills, techniques and procedures, BATSAC also teaches the general principles of Positive Teaching. This enables teachers to use positive methods creatively as well as being able to follow our proven procedures in appropriate situations. More specifically, the contingent and effective use of praise is emphasised. Teachers are also taught related skills such as effective rule setting, whilst video-tapes of classes are used to train teachers in how to "catch them being good" (i.e. to find appropriate times for praise). Various techniques are practised by which teacher praise can be increased and made more effective.

BATSAC has been subject to continual and continuing change and modification during its development. We will not detail the changes here but BATSAC progressed through several revisions before we were sufficiently satisfied to release it for more general use. All teachers who have taken part in BATSAC courses so far have helped in its evaluation and, hence, its development. Since our aim has been to train teachers to be more positive the main focus of our attempts at evaluation has been to see, quite simply, whether BATSAC does, in fact, bring about change in teacher behaviour.

We would first like to summarise the feedback we received from participants on five recent BATSAC courses. We analysed evaluation forms from 54 teachers who had attended these courses. The first question on the evaluation form (which is completed anonymously) asks teachers to compare their attitudes towards BATSAC prior to and after the course. Whereas 48% said that they had held favourable or very favourable attitudes before the course after the course this figure had risen to 96%. The vast majority of teachers (94%) also said that they would recommend a colleague to attend a BATSAC course. Most teachers (87%) believed that they had increased their use of approval whilst 63% felt that they had decreased their use of negative responses. Finally, 85% claimed to be more aware of children's behaviour and 89% claimed to be more aware of their own behaviour.

These results suggest a high degree of teacher satisfaction with the course but we also needed to know whether BATSAC really did change teachers' and, hence, pupils' classroom behaviour. Consequently, succeeding versions of BATSAC were piloted in two independent studies. The first study was carried out with all nine staff of a maths department in a secondary school. Teachers and their classes were observed, on three occasions, before and after attending the course. Teachers' use of disapproval decreased significantly but teacher approval was not appreciably affected. Clearly, though, by reducing the negatives, we had brought about an important shift in the ratio of positives to negatives. As we have stressed repeatedly, getting this response ratio shifted to the positive side is the key to success. All the teachers, except one, substantially improved their response ratios. As a consequence, the on-task behaviour levels of the classes they taught increased by 18% on average, ranging from 6% to 30%.

In the second study, a much improved version of BATSAC was employed with a group of 14 teachers and their classes in another secondary school and again teachers and pupils were observed before and after the course. In this study teacher approval increased, use of disapproval decreased and pupil on-task behaviour increased, all results being highly significant. This time all the teachers greatly improved their response ratios and levels of on-task behaviour in all classes improved by an average of 11%, ranging from 5% to 19%. It should be noted, however, that the average on-task levels for the classes taught by these teachers were already 78% before the course began, whereas, in the first study on-task levels had been much lower, averaging only 62%. In other words, there was more room for improvement in the first study.

These results were very encouraging. As a result of these experimental studies and teacher feedback we believe that we now have a much improved version of BATSAC which clearly changes teacher behaviour and which we have now made available to trained tutors.

BATSAC was designed specifically to help teachers with general problems of classroom management in mainstream secondary schools. However, one of the major concerns of many teachers is the presence of one or two really troublesome pupils. Such children can be very disruptive and cause a great deal of trouble to an already harassed teacher. This is the reason that BATSAC concentrates upon dealing with the class as a whole for we would argue that with good general classroom management the problems raised by pupils who are especially troublesome are much more manageable. Nevertheless, the problem pupils, like the poor, will always be with us and so we are beginning to develop a further package to help secondary teachers deal with them, currently codenamed BRATPACK!

The Elton Report and subsequent policy decisions made by the Secretary of State for Education and Science have stressed the importance of effective classroom behaviour management in relation to the professional competence of teachers. Strong recommendations have been about the provision of training for teachers in this area both at pre-service and in-service levels. In this book we have tried to convince readers of the benefits of Positive Teaching in relation to effective classroom behaviour management. We have discussed the basic operating principles, we have described our surveys and observational studies and we have reported numerous demonstration studies of Positive Teaching in practice in the classroom. We hope that reading this book will whet your appetite for Positive Teaching but reading is no substitute for doing. So why not put Positive Teaching to the test? Try it out for yourself in class!

Further reading

The study on pupil self-recording is described fully in:

Merrett, F. and Blundell, D. (1982). Self-recording as a means of improving classroom behaviour in the secondary school. *Educational Psychology, 2,* 147-157.

The studies on RPI with secondary pupils are reported in :

Wheldall, K. and Merrett, F. (1985). Reducing troublesome behaviour in the secondary school. *Maladjustment and Therapeutic Education, 3,* (2), 37-46.

Wheldall, K. and Merrett, F. (1987). What is the behavioural approach to teaching? In Hastings, N. and Schwieso, J. (eds) *New Directions in Educational Psychology II: behaviour and motivation.* London: Falmer Press.

Numerous case-studies of interventions carried out by teachers in their own classrooms using Positive Teaching methods are described in:

Merrett, F. E. (1986). *Encouragement Works Better Than Punishment* (second edition). Birmingham: Positive Products.

The development of the Positive Teaching training packages is described in:

Wheldall, K. and Merrett, F. (1987). Training teachers to use the behavioural approach to classroom management: the development of BATPACK. In Wheldall, K. (ed.) *The Behaviourist in the Classroom.* London: Allen & Unwin.

Wheldall, K. and Merrett, F. (1988). Packages for training teachers in classroom behaviour management: BATPACK, BATSAC and the Positive Teaching Packages. *Support for Learning, 3,* 86-92.

INDEX